Tanya B. Ditto

English
Springer Spaniels

A Complete Pet Owner's Manual

With 35 Color Photographs
34 Drawings by Michele Earle-Bridges

Consulting Editor: Matthew M. Vriends, Ph.D.

D0963250

BARRON'S

About the Author:

Tanya Brady Ditto, a member of Dog Writers' Association of America, last year won that organization's annual writing competition for her Barron's book, *Shar-Pei, A Complete Pet Owner's Manual.* She is also the author of Barron's *Dalmatians.* Mrs. Ditto and her husband, Bill, live in Springdale, Arkansas.

All inquiries should be addressed to:
Barron's Educational Series, Inc.
250 Wireless Boulevard
Hauppauge, New York 11788

International Standard Book No. 0-8120-1778-1

Library of Congress Catalog Card No. 93-44394

Library of Congress Cataloging-in-Publication Data

Ditto, Tanya B.
    English springer spaniels / Tanya B. Ditto.
        p.   cm. — (A Complete pet owner's manual)
    Includes bibliographical references (p. 87) and index.
    ISBN 0-8120-1778-1
    1. English springer spaniels. I. Title. II. Series.
SF429.E7D57   1994   93-44394
636.7'52—dc20   CIP

PRINTED IN HONG KONG
67 9927 987

Photo Credits:

Michele Earle Bridges: inside front cover, pages 27 (top left), 28, 63 (bottom left), back cover (bottom right); Gary Ellis: page 9 (bottom); Susan Green: pages 9 (top), 63 (top), back cover (top right); Judith Strom: front cover, pages 10, 27 (top right, bottom), 45, 46, 63 (bottom right), 64, back cover (top right, bottom right).

Advice and Warning:

This book is concerned with selecting, keeping, and raising English springer spaniels. The publisher and the author think it is important to point out that the advice and information for springer spaniel maintenance applies to healthy, normally developed animals. Anyone who acquires an adult dog or one from an animal shelter must consider that the animal may have behavioral problems and may, for example, bite without any visible provocation. Such anxiety-biters are dangerous for the owners as well as the general public.

Caution is further advised in the association of children with dogs, in meetings with other dogs, and in exercising the dog without a leash.

Contents

Preface

For countless years the springer spaniel has been "top dog" in homes and fields around the world. In addition to pleasant personal experiences, it has been our pleasure to meet many of the breed's finest in the fading pages of timeless books. Although the authors of these stories and the springers that starred in them are gone, their exploits and shared heroisms remain with us, caught in the pages of these old-fashioned volumes waiting for us to find them again, and thus to learn.

Some of these out-of-print books are listed in the bibliography at the back of the text. Unfortunately, most are only available through diligent search of public libraries, breed clubs, or collectible bookstores. When you do, however, locate one of these ancient windows on the past, pause. Rest for a moment in a pleasant time when dogs and humankind lived together in peace. Together both were welcome in the finest homes, parks, restaurants, and shops of the world. These old books contain the memories of those friendships. I commend them to you.

The springer breeders and springer lovers of today keep the lines of communication open with an informative quarterly newsletter, *The Spotlight,* published by the English Springer Spaniel Field Trial Association. The bulletin's knowledgeable editors, Melodie Hanke and Peggy Johnson, willingly shared their historical resources with me. ESSFTA Membership Secretary Elaine Resner was most helpful in pointing me in the right direction. I do thank them.

My sincere thanks to Donald Mayfield, D.V.M., for his input on the health care chapters. Once again, thanks to Helgard Niewisch, D.V.M., for her straightforward and insightful comments. I am indebted to them.

Consultant Matthew Vriends, Editor Don Reis, and the keen-eyed copyeditors at Barron's deserve special mention for their professionalism and competence. I thank them for their help.

As always, Bill's sharp-eyed proofreading bluelined the verbal redundancies while his sharp-eyed mathematics converted pounds, kilos, meters, and tablespoonfuls into however many cupfuls of whatever that the text required. I appreciate him.

History of the Springer Spaniel

The springer spaniel is an ancient, affectionate breed hailed by centuries of sportsmen as an excellent hunter, but today it is as frequently found on the sofa as in the field. Owners praise the springer's loyalty and devotion. Bystanders admire its magnificent coat and those long, velvet ears. Trainers appreciate its intelligence and adaptability. With so many vocal supporters on all sides, it is small wonder that springers are among today's most sought-after breeds.

Origins and Early History

According to respected spaniel author and breed judge Maxwell Riddle, the first written reference to a spaniel occurred in Ireland in the year A.D. 17. At that time a scribe entered in the king's ledger a gift of "water spaniels." Riddle speculated that this admittedly bare reference was important beyond a simple evidence of breed existence. He pointed out that because the reference was to a specific type of spaniel, authorities already had recognized the breed's diversity and had accepted its variances.

How Did the Spaniels Get Their Name?

It is generally understood and accepted by the dog "fancy" (a fancy word for those who are fond of dogs) that the early spaniels originated in Spain. What can be hard for the newcomer to understand, however, is how dogs called spaniels can be of radically diverse sizes, or sport any of several colors. Bystanders wonder at spaniels that may or may not have the typically pendulous ears, and (most importantly for a renowned hunting breed) that may exhibit no more than a passing interest in field work.

One answer lies in antiquity. Historians speculate that Roman soldiers, on their marches through the far regions of the civilized world, helped spread various spaniel-like breeds throughout Europe. It seems likely that the soldiers, undoubtedly attracted to these amiable and companionable dogs of Spain, carried the puppies from the country as pets, as souvenirs, or as helpful meat-hunters. We assume that, whatever name the dogs had been called by in their home country, they were inadvertently renamed by their new owners. More than likely, those who inquired about the dogs were told they hailed from Hispania, the Roman word for Spain. Thus, assorted as the dogs' physical characteristics might have been, these long-haired, for the most part flop-eared, pets were thereafter collectively referred to as "the spaniels." To this day, the spaniels they remain.

The Spaniel Today

The English springer spaniel is one of 17 breeds of spaniels. In 1992, English springers were listed nineteenth in dogdom's annual popularity contest, (winners being determined by the number of dogs registered with the American Kennel Club.) They are outranked in the spaniel

The English springer spaniel, top dog in the home, in the show ring, and in the field.

family only by the cocker, which is third on the list behind the number one Labrador retrievers and second place rottweilers.

Spaniel lovers recognize two distinct types and sizes of spaniels as typical of the breed. Each type evolved from deliberate and selective mating designed to accomplish a particular purpose. The dogs known as "spaniels" can properly weigh from as little as 7 pounds (3.2 kg) to a respectable 65 pounds (29.5 kg) at maturity. Some spaniels are tall and rangy, others are heavy-set and short. Some are lightweight lapdogs. Others are relative giants.

Coat color is an important factor in most spaniels. Even here, however, important differences mark the breeds. Breeders highly prize the reddish coat color of Welsh springers, for instance. On the other hand, red is not an acceptable coat color for English springers.

Although our focus is on the English springer spaniel, we will for a moment consider the links of kinship in the background of this remarkably diverse breed.

The Nine Sporting Spaniels

Each of the sporting spaniels, a designation given to the springer and eight of its cousins, was bred for specific territorial needs. It would make sense that in some hunting ranges, and for some quarry, larger dogs with their greater stamina, were considered superior. The clumbers, the largest of all spaniels, and the Sussex, one of the oldest breeds, were developed for the purpose of hunting in dense terrain. Those bird hunters who also wanted spaniels as house pets preferred smaller spaniels and in time produced a line of sturdy hunting cockers.

English and Welsh Springers

Both the English and the Welsh springers undoubtedly are related closely. Both are medium-sized, compact dogs, greatly admired for their hunting abilities. Both are known for their trademark trait of "springing" at game. The Welsh springer's red and white coat is an outstanding characteristic of the breed.

Irish and American Water Spaniels

The Irish water spaniel is aptly named. Its love of water and its dense, oily coat, always solid liver in color, combine to produce a respected duck hunting companion. The American water spaniel, a fluffier dog than the Irish spaniel, also sports a dense, tightly curled coat. This spaniel, developed in the United States, is thought to be a result of breedings of Irish water spaniels and curly-coated retrievers.

American and English Cockers

Cockers were bred on both sides of the Atlantic. With the exception of blood lines, the strains show remarkable similarity. Some historians tell us that cockers derive their names from their skills at hunting woodcock, a small gamebird. Others, pointing to the older use of cocker as a word meaning to "indulge or pamper" suggest that the dog's amiable nature tempts its master to indulgence. Cockers are among the smallest of the sporting breeds, weighing at maturity about 25 pounds (11 kg).

Sussex, Field, and Clumber Spaniels

The Sussex spaniel is one of the oldest recognized spaniels. One authority, writing in 1805, suggests that the Sussex is basically a large cocker that was developed from strong, cocker lineage. It is only certain that this breed takes its name from Sussex, England, where it was a preferred hunting dog as long ago as the 1700s.

Field spaniels, among the rarest of the spaniels, were apparently produced from a cross of Sussex and cocker lines. The fields are medium-sized, solid-colored gundogs.

The massive clumber spaniels can properly weigh up to 65 pounds (29.5 kg). Bred to be strong gundogs able to work in dense underbrush, the clumber is long and low to the ground. It is sometimes described as the St. Bernard of spaniels.

The Eight Toy Spaniels

In the sixteenth century, several small spaniels so amused the ladies of the English court that the breed's popularity soared. These pampered and petted lapdogs slept next to, ate at the table with, and went riding alongside their mistresses. Rarely did the ladies allow their pets the run of the halls for fear of their being trampled, or worse, set upon by larger dogs. It became a habit for their mistresses to carry about these small, warm "comforter" spaniels nestled in a stomach snuggler, much the same carrier as is used for babies today. The practice also provided a little warmth for the ladies on chilly winter mornings.

The spaniel was such a hit in England that by the seventeenth century an assortment of spaniels accompanied King Charles II through the halls of his palaces. It is said that Charles, known as the Merry Monarch, not only allowed his dogs into his council meetings, but permitted his favorites to have their puppies in his bedroom.

The sporting instinct in the toy spaniels remains high. But, don't be misled by the word spaniel in their breed name and expect the toys to be active outdoor hunting dogs, albeit smaller. They are not. The toys love water and the outdoors as much as do their larger cousins, the sporting spaniels, but toys cannot handle much of either. Although the toys do retain much of their hunting instinct, and enjoy a bout with backyard squirrels and rabbits, for example, they are neither temperamentally nor physically suited for true hunting. These are tiny, sensitive bundles of energy that much prefer a chase through your pockets in search of a bit of cheese.

English Spaniels

Although their origin is undoubtedly Japanese, these bright-eyed so-called sleeve or lap dogs, have been known and loved in England and Scotland since the sixteenth century. Favored with blunt, upturned muzzles, the English spaniels gaze appealingly upward. Their typically large, black eyes and enormous pupils focus intently on their patrons. Bright and energetic, the English toy spaniels enjoy a pampered lifestyle and, in return, live up to their reputation as pleasant companions.

All five of the English spaniels mentioned next are closely related. Color variation is usually the key to identification.

King Charles and Ruby English Spaniels: The early spaniels favored by the seventeenth century Merry Monarch, and those that eventually received his name, were black-and-tan. Apparently several coat color mutations occurred through the years that eventually brought about the five varieties known today. Today, breed guidelines consider this black-and-tan dog a "solid" color because the mahogany tan coloration is limited to the muzzle, chest, and legs with some tan coloration over the prominent eyes.

The ruby spaniel, a rich chestnut red, is a solid color dog, with no markings. The ruby spaniel has a beautiful head, and like the other toys, sports long, ruffly feathered ears that occasionally reach 20 inches (51 cm) in length.

Blenheim and Prince Charles English Spaniels: It is said that the original breeding pair of what came to be known as Blenheims was a set of red-and-white cockers brought to England from China. Their coats are considered "broken-colored" (as opposed to the King Charles and the Ruby spaniels which are whole-colored). Both the Blenheim and the King Charles display an overlay of patches, either bright red chestnut or ruby-red, on a pearly white background. One distinctive and identifying feature of the Blenheim is a dime-sized spot of red at the top of its forehead.

History of the Springer Spaniel

The Prince Charles English spaniel is a tricolored dog of white, black, and tan. As in the Blenheims, the predominant color is usually pearly white, with the black scattered in patches. As in the King Charles, the tan is limited to an area above the eyes, on the muzzle, chest, and legs. One major distinction between the Prince Charles and the Blenheim is that the Prince Charles has no spot on its forehead.

Cavalier King Charles English Spaniels: The background coat color on the Cavalier can be a solid shiny red or a solid pearly white, but all Cavalier coats have markings of chestnut, black, or tan. Like the other toys, these pets are loving, affectionate, and perfectly suited for small living quarters.

Japanese Spaniel

Like its toy cousins, the Japanese spaniel (known also as the Japanese Chin) is an aristocratic oriental-looking dog, usually black and white. The Chin's alert eyes are large and prominent. Its plumed tail, which is a distinctive feature of the breed, is carried high. Introduced to the West in 1853 by Commodore Perry who presented several to Queen Victoria as gifts from the Emperor of Japan, the Chins have a stylish look about them that enhances their popularity.

Tibetan Spaniel

For centuries inhabitants of the isolated, mountainous country of Tibet had little contact with the outside world. When visitors did arrive, however, they were usually offered the hospitality of the monasteries and palaces. Following these visits the newcomers wrote admiringly of the catlike little spaniels of Tibet.

The history of the Tibetan spaniel is steeped in symbolism. In memory of the teachings of the Lord Buddha, who had tamed the lion to follow at his heels "like a faithful dog," the Tibetans referred to their loyal spaniels as "little lions."

Hence the term *lion dog* has accompanied the breed to this day. On their departure the visitors were occasionally presented with these affectionate, light-eyed spaniels as symbols of peace and friendship.

Papillon

The Papillon, or continental toy spaniel, does not have the hanging ears typical of the spaniel family. Instead, its erect, feathered ears are held upright. When in motion, the ears remind the observer of the spread wings of a butterfly, hence its name. (*Papillon* means "butterfly" in French.) This well-liked little spaniel is thought to be a descendant of the fifteenth century spaniels that peer from paintings on museum walls today. These pampered pets are often portrayed nestled in the laps or at the feet of their rich and famous owners as they obediently posed for the portraits that we still admire.

The Springer, Top Dog

The English springer spaniel, as we have seen, has 16 first cousins, and each breed has its own cheerleaders. If you would like to pursue your interest, breed clubs will share their information. Newcomers are always welcome at club gatherings and shows. Any of the breed clubs can be contacted for literature and for information. Addresses can be obtained from the American Kennel Club.

The springer, however, which is top dog in this book, has its own cheerleaders in some pretty

Top: Making one selection from a perfect litter can be a lot of fun.
Bottom: The breed's placid disposition and appealing gaze ensure its reputation as a lovable pet.

fancy places. Want a dog that can write a best-seller? One of today's springer's did just that when Millie, "The White House Dog," coauthored a memoir with the help of her owner, former First Lady Barbara Bush. Proceeds from the First Dog's unabashedly immodest account are donated to the Barbara Bush Foundation for Family Literacy.

One of the premier honors in the world of dogs was bestowed on a springer in Madison Square Garden in early February, 1993. English springer spaniel Champion Salilyn's Condor (nicknamed Robert) having previously won the Sporting Dog Group, was awarded Best in Show at the 117th Westminster Kennel Club Show in New York City. The honor was well deserved and well received by the audience. Although each of the Group winners was of superior quality and had survived rigorous competition all week, the judge gave the final honor to the springer, saying, "I was blessed with many good specimens. I think the dog that won it is a great dog. Last night was his finest hour."

Perhaps you already own a springer. Maybe you still are considering a purchase. This book is designed to help you make the right decisions as you travel the long road of friendship together. Keep the book handy and refer to it when you have a question. Be observant. Have fun. Have confidence that as you and your springer take those first steps of friendship together your own finest hours lie ahead.

Top: Sunshine and springtime showcase the litter's top form.
Bottom left: Sometimes enthusiasm for that elusive odor supplants a participant's better judgment.
Bottom right: Now where did that shoelace go? Anybody see that shoe?

Understanding Springer Spaniels

Understanding Dogs

Eons ago, humans and dogs embarked upon a mutually beneficial journey that culminated in a centuries-long friendship. That friendship was forged with trust, sharing, and an endless ability to forgive.

Writers through the ages composed poems, essays, speeches, and epitaphs honoring their faithful friends that had passed on. Although this praise and respect, often honoring the dog's unconditional loyalty and steadfast courage, comes to all breeds, that for the spaniel is unsurpassed.

Many poets, among them Alexander Pope, William Wordsworth, and Lord Byron eulogized their faithful pets. Some, sorrowing over a loss, expressed gratitude for friendship shared, and offered hope that human being and dog would meet again.

Others—like humorists James Thurber, Will Rogers, and Dave Barry—vented their good-natured exasperation with their pets in tongue-in-cheek essays.

Geoffrey Chaucer, a fourteenth century story-teller, referred to a "spaynel" dog. The dog was described as liking to "lepe" at people. A spaynel related to our "springer," perhaps?

Optimists (poet Elizabeth Barrett Browning comes to mind) have spent countless hours trying to communicate with their pets, to bridge that last void between dog and humanity. They see, as do many of us, an awareness and a native intelligence behind those liquid eyes, an intelligence that author Jack London called "beyond mere words."

Housebound and lonesome, Miss Barrett hoped that her cocker spaniel, Flush, could learn to play dominoes with her. She therefore worked diligently to teach Flush to count. In letters to her friends, Miss Barrett outlined her plan and sent periodic progress reports. To her dismay, Flush apparently never learned to count beyond "three" and the plan for dominoes had to be abandoned. Eventually, not deterred by Flush's lack of mathematical skills, she tried to teach Flush the alphabet, but finally wrote in despair to one friend, "he has no very pronounced love for literature." No doubt throughout their lives together both the poet and Flush continued their efforts to communicate.

Many years ago, the poet and playwright Maurice Maeterlinck reminded us of just how unique is the friendship between man and dog. Maeterlinck's eulogy to "Our Friend the Dog," was written in memory of his six-month-old bulldog puppy, Pelleas. In his essay, Maeterlinck observes that of all the species on earth, only the dog stands by our side, and because he has chosen to do so, effectively deserts the whole animal kingdom to which he belongs.

The dog, Maeterlinck writes, is born instinctively willing to be our friend. "Amid all the forms of life that surround us, not one, excepting the dog, has made an alliance with us. Many creatures fear us, most are unaware of us, and none unselfishly love us."

That the dog remains our friend through all the changes and transformations we have instituted to help him meet our own needs, is a tribute to its tenacity. In humanity's search for the perfect companion and helper, we have even altered the dog's shape as we developed guard dogs that possess stronger jaws, hunting dogs that display greater lung power, northern dogs endowed with heavier fur, and toy dogs that fit into our pockets.

This enduring friendship, as Maeterlinck observed, is unusual. Most of the other animals on earth seem to regard humans as little more than caretakers. These species equally have little to do with other animals, except perhaps to view them as objects in the food chain. The devoted dog remains the only animal that has, as the essay tells us, "crossed the enormous zone of darkness, ice, and silence...escaping from itself to come bounding toward us, (and) given himself to man."

Understanding Springer Spaniels

These authors used language to depict people's fascination with dogs. Artists expressed their appreciation of Man's Best Friend in murals, wall hangings, and sculpture.

For centuries, animal lovers commissioned portraits of their family pets, thereby honoring the years of loyalty, or celebrating the courage and the hunting skills of their companions. Wealthy families often included the family dog in group portraits destined for the mantle. Many of these paintings hang in permanent exhibit in galleries. Many more, whether paintings or photographs, hang in places of honor in homes such as yours and mine.

Fidelity

Loyalty and trustworthiness are two of the most appreciated characteristics of dogs. Through the centuries, the dog most admired for these qualities was called Argus. Over twenty-five hundred years ago, the poet Homer told an unforgettable tale of fidelity.

It seems that, having been away for many years, the traveler Ulysses returned to his home. He had been gone for so long, though, that everyone who had known him—his friends, his servants, and his family—agreed he must be dead. When Ulysses arrived at the door, no one recognized him and he was turned away. As Ulysses left, he walked by his old dog Argus, the companion of his youth. Argus, now lame and almost blind, had waited all these years for Ulysses to return. When the dog heard his master's voice it crept forward. Ulysses knelt to pet his old friend, and Argus died in his arms, faithful to the end. At that point the members of the household also recognized Ulysses and rushed out to welcome him home.

Humanity's Helper

The dog has assisted humans in numerous ways through the centuries of their friendship.

From the beginning, man and dog hunted together to provide food for the family. If an arrow missed its mark, the dog retrieved the arrow. If the arrow hit or wounded its target, the dog retrieved the game.

In the intervening centuries, dogs have learned to carry messages, to guard property, to search debris for victims, and to play the circus clown. Today, dogs perform services to disabled people, enabling many to lead productive and independent lives. Many dogs are part of therapy groups visiting hospitals and nursing homes as part of a nationwide program reaching out to shut-ins.

Understanding Your Springer

The English springer spaniel is an alert, intelligent dog deserving of the title all-around companion. Few spaniels can top the English

A fenced yard provides safety for springers and peace of mind for those who love them.

springer's superior athletic ability. A respected hunting dog, a bird hunter with few equals, the springer has a competitive spirit capable of earning honors in the field, in the show ring, and in your heart.

External Appearance

The first thing most people notice about a springer is the beautiful, pendulous ears well covered with fine feathered hair. In addition to their handsome appearance, the ears, set at about eye level, also perform the functional service of protecting the dog from water.

A springer is bred with a good, heavy muzzle, and long, muscular neck, specifically intended to help him retrieve game. Hunters like to say that "A springer grasps with the teeth but weight is borne by the neck."

The springer coat is of many colors, dense enough to be waterproof and thornproof, but light enough to be glossy and refined in texture.

The springer should measure 18 to 22 inches (45–55 cm) high at the shoulder, and weigh between 40 to 50 pounds (18–22 kg). Its overall appearance should give the onlooker an instant impression of the grace and stamina of the breed.

The English Springer Spaniel Field Trial Association (ESSFTA) writes and the American Kennel Club (AKC) endorses a breed Standard that serves as a guideline for breeders and judges. As of this writing a proposed revision of the latest Standard, which coordinates several items, eliminates redundancies, and clarifies matters of gait, size, bite, and temperament, is under consideration. The revised standard is expected to receive approval and be in place in 1994. Until such time the following explanation and condensation can be used as a guide. For the latest official Standard, contact the ESSFTA at the address listed in the back pages of this book.

General Appearance and Type

The English springer spaniel is a medium-sized sporting dog with a neat, compact body and a docked tail. Its coat is moderately long and glossy with feathering on the legs, ears, chest, and brisket. Its pendulous ears, soft gentle expression, sturdy build, and friendly wagging tail proclaim it unmistakably a member of the ancient family of spaniels. It is above all a well-proportioned dog, free from exaggeration, nicely balanced in every part. Its carriage is proud and upstanding, body deep, legs strong and muscular with enough length to carry it with ease. Taken as a whole, the English springer spaniel suggests power, endurance, agility. It looks the part of a dog that can go and keep going under difficult hunting conditions: moreover it thoroughly enjoys such activity. At its best it is endowed with style, symmetry, balance, enthusiasm, and is every inch a sporting dog of distinct spaniel character, combining beauty and utility.

Size, Proportion, and Substance: The springer is built to cover rough ground with agility and reasonable speed. Its body structure suggests the capacity for endurance. It should be kept to medium size, neither too small nor too large and heavy to do the work for which the breed is intended. The ideal shoulder height for dogs is 20 inches (50 cm); for bitches, 19 inches (48 cm). Those more than 1 inch (2.5 mm) under or over the breed ideal are to be faulted. Weight is dependent on the dog's other dimensions: a 20-inch (50 cm) dog, well proportioned, in good condition, should weigh approximately 50 pounds (22 kg). A 19-inch bitch will weigh approximately 40 pounds (18 kg). The length of the body (measured from point of shoulder to point of buttocks) is slightly greater than the height at the withers. The dog too long in body, especially when long in loin, tires easily and lacks the compact outline characteristic of the breed. Equally undesirable is the dog too short in body for the length of its legs, a condition that destroys balance and restricts the

The springer's sturdy bone structure encourages its erect carriage.

The well-muscled English springer can hunt for hours without tiring.

gait. A springer with correct substance is a well-knit and sturdy dog with good but not too heavy bone, in no way coarse or ponderous.

Color: (1) May be black or liver with white markings or predominantly white with black or liver markings; (2) blue or liver roan, (3) tricolor: black and white or liver and white with tan markings (usually found on eyebrows, cheeks, inside of ears and under tail); any white portions of coat may be flecked with ticking. All preceding combinations of colors and markings are equally acceptable. Off colors such as lemon, red, or orange are faults.

Coat: The springer has an outercoat and an undercoat. The outercoat is flat or wavy, of medium length, and is easily distinguishable from the undercoat which is short, soft, and dense. The quantity of undercoat is affected by climate and season. In combination, outercoat and undercoat serve to make the dog substantially waterproof, weatherproof, and thornproof. In ears, chest, legs, and belly the springer is nicely furnished with a fringe of feathering of moderate length and heavi-

ness. On the head, front of forelegs, and below the hock joints on the front of the hindlegs the hair is short and fine. The coat has the clean, glossy, "live" appearance indicative of good health. It is legitimate to trim around the head, neck, feet, and ears to remove dead hair and to thin and shorten excess feathering particularly from the hocks to the feet as required to give a smart, functional appearance. Overtrimming, especially of the body coat, or any chopped, barbered, or artificial effect is penalized in the show ring, as is excessive feathering that destroys the clean outline desirable in a sporting dog. Correct quality and condition of coat takes precedence over quantity of coat.

Head: The head is impressive without being heavy. Its beauty lies in a combination of strength and refinement. It is important that the size and proportion be in balance with the rest of the dog. Viewed in profile the head should appear approximately the same length as the neck and should blend with the body in substance.

More than any other feature the eyes contribute to the springer's appeal. The stop, eyebrows, and

Understanding Springer Spaniels

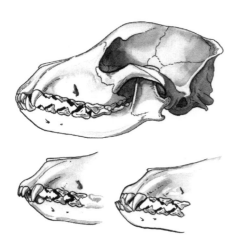

The English springer's teeth correctly meet in a scissor's bite, at top. The overbite (left) and underbite (right) are considered faults.

chiseling of the bony structure around the eye sockets contribute to the springer's beautiful and characteristic expression, which is alert, kindly, and trusting. Color, placement, and size influence expression and attractiveness. The eyes are to be of medium size and oval in shape, neither small, round, full and prominent, nor bold and hard in expression, they are set rather well apart and fairly deep in their sockets. The color of the iris is to harmonize with the color of the coat, preferably a good dark hazel in the liver dogs and black or deep brown in the black and white specimens.

The skull (upper head) is of medium length, fairly broad, flat on top, slightly rounded at the sides and back. The occiput bone is inconspicuous, rounded rather than peaked or angular. The foreface (head in front of the eyes) is approximately the same length as the skull, and in harmony as to width and general character. Looking down on the head, the muzzle appears to be about one half the width of the skull. As the skull rises from the foreface it makes a brow or "stop,"

divided by a groove or fluting between the eyes. This groove continues upward and gradually disappears as it reaches the middle of the forehead. The amount of "stop" can best be described as moderate. It must not be a pronounced feature; rather, it is a subtle rise where the muzzle blends into the upper head, further emphasized by the groove and by the position and shape of the eyebrows which should be well developed. The stop, eyebrow, and chiseling of the bony structure around the eye sockets contribute to the springer's beautiful and characteristic expression.

Viewed in profile the topline of the skull and muzzle lie in two approximately parallel planes. The nasal bone should be straight, with no downward inclination toward the tip of the nose which gives a downfaced look undesirable in this breed. Neither should the nasal bone be concave resulting in a dish-faced profile; nor convex giving the dog a Roman nose. The jaws must be of sufficient length to allow the dog to carry game easily; fairly square, lean, strong, and even (neither undershot nor overshot). The upper lip is not pendulous or exaggerated. The nostrils are well opened and broad, liver color or black depending on the color of the coat. Flesh-colored ("Dudley noses"), or spotted ("butterfly noses") are undesirable. The cheeks are to be flat (not rounded, full, or thick) with nice chiseling under the eyes. Faults that are to be penalized are oval, pointed, or heavy skull; prominently rounded, thick, and protruding cheeks; too much or too little stop; too heavy, too short, too thick, or too narrow a muzzle; and pendulous, slobbery lips. Under- or over-shot jaws are a very serious fault that is heavily penalized.

Teeth: The teeth should be strong, clean, not too small, and when the mouth is closed the teeth should meet in a closed scissors bite (the lower incisors touching the inside of the upper incisors). An even bite or one or two incisors slightly out of line are minor faults.

Ears: The ears must be set on a level with the line of the eye, on the side of the skull, and not too far back. The flaps need to be long and fairly wide, hanging close to the cheeks, with no tendency to stand up or out; the leather must be thin and approximately long enough to reach the tip of the nose.

Neck: The neck is moderately long, muscular, slightly arched at the crest, and gradually blends into sloping shoulders.

Body: The body is short-coupled, strong, compact; the chest is deep but not so wide or round as to interfere with the action of the front legs; the brisket is sufficiently developed to reach to the level of the elbows. The ribs are fairly long, springing gradually to the middle of the body then tapering as they approach the end of the ribbed section. The back (section between the withers and loin) is straight, strong, and essentially level, with no tendency to dip or roach. The loins are strong and short; a slight arch shows over loins and hip bones. Hips are nicely rounded and blend smoothly into hind legs. The resulting topline slopes very gently from withers to tail—the line from withers to back descending without a sharp drop; the back practically level; arch over hips somewhat lower than the withers; croup sloping gently to base of tail; tail carried to follow the natural line of the body. The underline, starting on a level with the elbows, constitutes backward with almost no up-curve until reaching the end of the ribbed section, then a more noticeable up-curve to the flank, but not enough to make the dog appear small waisted or "tucked-up."

Tail: The springer's tail is an index both to his temperament and his conformation. Merry tail action is characteristic. The proper set is somewhat low following the natural line of the croup. The carriage should be nearly horizontal, slightly elevated when the dog is excited. Carried straight up is untypical of the breed. The tail should not be docked too short and should be well fringed with wavy feather. It is legitimate to shape and shorten the feathering, but enough should be left to blend with the dog's other furnishings. Faults that are to

be penalized include a tail habitually upright, a tail set too high, or too low. A clamped down tail (indicating timidity or undependable temperament) is even less to be desired than a tail carried too gaily and is to be faulted as is a tail carried at a right angle to the backline in terrier fashion.

Forequarters: Efficient movement in front calls for proper shoulder assembly; the shoulder blades need to be flat and fairly close together at the tips, molding smoothly into the contour of the body. Ideally, when measured from the top of the withers to the point of the shoulder to the elbow, the shoulder blade and upper arm are of apparent equal length, forming an angle of nearly 90 degrees; this sets the front legs well under the body and places the elbows directly beneath the tips of the shoulder blades. Elbows lie close to the body with free action from the shoulders. Forelegs are straight and of equal length to the foot. The leg bone appears strong, slightly flattened, not too heavy or round. The knees are straight, almost flat; the pasterns, short, strong, and slightly sloping, with no suggestion of weakness.

Hindquarters: The springer should look hard and muscular with well-developed hips and broad thighs; its entire rear assembly should suggest strength and driving power. Stifle joints are strong. For functional efficiency the angulation of the hindquarter is never greater than that of the forequarter, and not appreciably less. The hock joint is somewhat rounded, not small and sharp in contour. Rear pasterns are short—about one-third the distance from hip joint to foot—and strong, with good bone; when viewed from the rear, they are parallel. Dewclaws are usually removed.

Feet: Feet are round or slightly oval. They are compact and well arched, of medium size with thick pads, and well feathered between the toes.

Movement: In judging the springer there should be emphasis on proper movement, which is the final test of a dog's conformation and soundness. Prerequisite to good movement is balance of front and rear assemblies. The two must

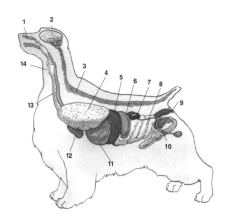

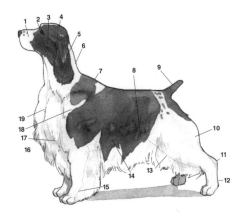

Internal Organs: 1. Nasal Sinus Cavity; 2. Brain; 3. Spinal Cord; 4. Lungs; 5. Stomach; 6. Spleen; 7. Kidneys; 8. Intestine; 9. Rectum; 10. Bladder; 11. Liver; 12. Heart; 13. Trachea; 14. Larynx.

Parts of the Dog: 1. Muzzle; 2. Stop; 3. Cheek; 4. Skull; 5. Ear; 6. Neck; 7. Withers; 8. Loin; 9. Tail; 10. Hindquarters; 11. Hock; 12. Rear Pastern; 13. Stifle; 14. Rib Cage; 15. Front Pastern; 16. Forequarters; 17. Chest; 18. Shoulder; 19. Brisket.

match in angulation and muscular development if the gait is to be smooth and effortless. Good shoulders laid back at an angle that permits a long stride are just as essential as the excellent rear quarters that provide the driving power. When viewed from the front, the dog's legs should appear to swing forward in a free and easy manner, with no tendency for the feet to cross over or interfere with each other. Viewed from the rear, the hocks should drive well under the body following on a line with the forelegs, neither too widely nor too closely spaced. As speed increases there is a natural tendency for the legs to converge toward the center line of gravity or a single line of travel. Seen from the side, the springer should exhibit a good, long, forward stride, without high-stepping or wasted motion. Faults that are penalized include: a short, choppy stride, mincing steps with up and down movement, hopping; moving with forefeet wide apart, giving a roll or swing to the body; weaving or crossing the fore or hind-feet; and hocks turning in toward each other, called cow-hocks.

Temperament: The typical springer is friendly, eager to please, quick to learn, willing to obey. In the show ring it should exhibit poise, attentiveness, tractability, and should permit close examination by the judge without showing resentment or cringing. Aggression toward people and aggression toward other dogs is not in keeping with the sporting dog character and purpose and is not acceptable. Excessive timidity, with due allowance for puppies and novice dogs, is equally penalized.

Summary: In evaluating the English springer spaniel, the overall picture is a primary consideration. The judges look for *type*, which includes general appearance, outline, and temperament; and also, for *soundness*, especially as seen when the dog is in motion. A spaniel with a smooth easy gait that is reasonably sound and well balanced is to be highly regarded in the show ring, but not to the extent of forgiving the dog for not looking like an English springer spaniel. A quite untypical dog—leggy, foreign in head and expression—may move well, but he should not be placed over

Understanding Springer Spaniels

a good all-around specimen that has a minor fault in movement. A judge must remember that the English springer spaniel is first and foremost a sporting dog of the spaniel family and he must *look, behave, and move* in character.

Coat Colors

The springer's myriad coat colors enable most breed enthusiasts to appreciate the uniformity of the breed, yet select the color they prefer. English springers are basically bicolored or tricolored dogs on a black, white, or liver background.

The basic background coats can be spotted, ticked, or roaned. (A coat is ticked if small, isolated areas of color show up on a white background. A roaned coat contains a fine mixture of colored hairs interspersed with white hairs.)

The following six springer coat colors are acceptable:
• Black with white markings
• Black with white and tan markings
• White with liver markings
• White with black markings
• Liver with white markings
• Liver with white and tan markings

Breed Attributes

In his *The Springer Spaniel* written in 1951, Maxwell Riddle called the springer "the world's best all-purpose dog." This respected breed judge pointed out the fact that the springer is "a moderately-sized dog, with good sense and quiet manners" at home, capable of hunting all day alone or in field trials, and frequently earning dual championship honors in conformation shows.

Since that book was written, breed expectations have undergone some changes, primarily concerning dual-purpose springers. Possibly because fewer hunters are taking to the field, or because the springer's charm has allowed it to enter the house

and stay in the house, many of today's springers are limited to hunting backyard squirrels.

Temperament

Much has been written of the springer's gentle temperament. Breeders and sportsmen have often praised the springer as active, easily trainable, and nonaggressive. This grassroots assessment was recently confirmed by a study conducted by two veterinarians working at the University of California. Dr. Benjamin Hart and Dr. Lynette Hart solicited and evaluated opinions from breeders, judges, professional handlers, and veterinarians on 56 dog breeds of which the springer was one.

The responses were then divided into categories that rated each breed's reactivity (its excitability and demand for attention), its dominance and aggression toward humans and other dogs, its trainability in terms of obedience and housetraining, and an analysis of both its destructive and its playful qualities.

On a scale ranging from low to medium to high the English springer spaniel was assessed as high in reactivity, as only medium in aggressiveness, and as very high in trainability. The evaluations confirmed what owners have been saying all along: The springer is a great hunting companion, a good friend, and a capable guard dog.

Nevertheless, prospective owners should be aware that some springer lines (as well as some lines of other breeds) carry a genetic disposition for what is called Rage syndrome. Basically, an afflicted dog has a sudden and incomprehensibly violent tantrum that seems schizophrenic in terms of the dog's ordinary behavior. Mild mannered pets inexplicably attack the living room sofa, the kennel walls, or, tragically, the owners or their children. The abnormal behavior ceases as mysteriously as it began. Rage syndrome is covered in greater depth in the section on Hereditary Problems in the Chapter, Keeping Your Springer Healthy (see page 77).

Retrieving and Tracking

Most springers love water. Few are gun shy, making them excellent hunting companions. Indeed, springers are thought to show more versatility in their hunting abilities than other gundogs. Although primarily bred as a pheasant hunter, the springer is equally capable when hunting rabbits, quail, partridge, and ducks.

Its keen sense of smell enables the springer to follow old body-scent tracks as well as dirty tracks (trails recently hunted by other dogs). Even as puppies, some springers are rarely stopped by a fence; they either climb over it or search for a way around it when on a trail.

The English springer is a duck dog. It loves the water, loves the chase, and loves being out of doors. It has a highly developed sense of smell that can follow the footfall of game and track it to its source. Its two-layer coat enables the springer to be comfortable on drizzly winter mornings as well as on humid summer afternoons.

Family Pet

The springer is amiable, affectionate, and good tempered. Although bred for the outdoors, it can, with proper attention and exercise, adapt to life in an apartment or suburban home.

Guard Dog

Perhaps the springer is not as protective of its perimeters as some breeds, but it is nevertheless a good watchdog. Both friends and strangers find their arrival announced long before they approach the front door. Ever loyal to its family, a properly trained springer will assume the role of yard sitter to the children of the house.

Communicating with Your Springer

Dogs understand a limited number of words and phrases. Experts set the number at twelve or fewer. Some owners claim that their dogs understand over a hundred words and phrases. However extensive the vocabulary claimed, all agree on one thing: what is most important is not what you say but how you say it. Words intended to be commands or instructions should be short, preferably one syllable, and decisively spoken. Commands accompanied by hand gestures and your own body language are the most effective of all.

How to Speak Dog

If you wish your dog, Brownie, to stop, for instance, telling her to "Stay!" while lifting a palm in imitation of a traffic patrol's gesture for stop, is more effective than the spoken word alone.

Although television shows occasionally feature dogs that "talk," "sing," or "count," such entertaining displays require a certain indulgence on the part of the observer. What the animals have exhibited is a desire to please their owners. Your dog "talks" to you by barking, whining, growling, or other verbalizations. The following list contains some of the most common meanings:

Growling: If soft and understated can mean, "Back off, I'm tired (sleepy, hungry)." If harsh and sharp, "Stop! Don't do that anymore!"

Barking: If the barking is in rapid sequence, one bark right after another, the dog might be telling you "I've encountered an unusual situation, come and see." Of course, an unusual situation can mean anything from the presence of an intruder, to a full moon rising, to conversing with other dogs, to a desire to root out rooting armadillos.

Whimpering: Usually means "I'm scared, I'm lonely," or "I'm hurt." A whimper that is more a whine often means, "I need to go out. Stop the car (or Open the house door)."

Body Language

Your dog, Brownie, also "talks" to you and to other animals by a sequence of body signals common to all breeds. Some of these easily read communications are:

Staring: If your own dog stares at you while you are trying to discipline it, it is sending a confrontational signal. Stare back and do not be the first one to look away. If an unfamiliar dog sends this signal with accompanying aggressive sounds, don't stare back. Avoid eye contact. In other words, if a dog attempts to "stare you down" and that stare is accompanied by other signs of aggression, do not accept the challenge. Leave the area.

Tail-Wagging: If Brownie wags her tail she is offering a friendly greeting. Conversely, if a dog holds its body stiffly and stands with its tail stiff and straight, the dog is ready to make or accept a challenge.

Crouching: If Brownie or any other dog assumes a crouching position, almost taking a bow with her front legs forward and her head lowered, she is inviting you to play.

Lying on back: If Brownie lies on her back at your feet, exposing her stomach, she is showing submission to your authority.

The Springer and Children

Few of us want to kennel our springers full time. Indeed, even those owners and their pets involved in hunting, dog shows, or field trials, recognize the value of close contact between the animals and their human families. At the end of the day many wind up in the kitchen, or in front of the television set with the family.

The springer loves attention. It will lie down and stretch to full body length for anyone will-ing to scratch its belly or its sides, or tickle it under the chin. Conversely, it will be a willing companion in countless games of fetch and run. Brownie will bound out the door ahead of you, and run back as if to say, "Why are you so slow? Let's go!"

Terms You Should Know

bitch: A female dog.

brisket: The part of the body below the chest, between the forelegs, closest to the ribs.

cow-hocks: When the hocks turn toward each other.

dog: A male dog; also used collectively to designate both male and female.

haw: A third eyelid or membrane in the inside corner of the eye.

hock: The dog's true heel.

leather: The flap of the ear.

loin: Region of the body between the last ribs and the hindquarters.

pastern: That part of the foreleg between the wrist and the toes.

roach back: A convex curve of the back.

scissors bite: The outside of the lower teeth touch the inside of the upper teeth.

stifle: The dog's knee.

topline: From just behind the withers to the tail set.

withers: The highest point of the shoulder.

Small children, of course, must learn how to maneuver around a large dog. Monitor the child's behavior until you are sure all is well. Teach the child to respect the dog and to recognize when the dog has had enough.

You will find that the springer is amazingly forgiving of small mistakes. It is also wise enough to leave an uncomfortable situation. If Brownie comes to you followed by a complaining child trying to hold on to her tail, listen to her side of it. Distract the child and separate the two for awhile. Even an easygoing springer like Brownie needs a break.

The Springer and Other Pets

There shouldn't be any problem associated with introducing a springer to other household pets. Springers have been known to share their quarters with cats, puppies, and other breeds.

It will be easier for you to bring a new puppy into the house than a full grown dog. Wise owners introduce a new pet slowly and affectionately. You will find that female dogs are often more territorial than the males, frequently resisting and often terrorizing a newcomer.

If you live or visit in the country, you would probably not want to give your springers the run of a yard inhabited by turkeys, chickens, or other feathered fowl. In the same vein, a farm pond filled with chattering, preening waterfowl is just a big playpen for a springer. You wouldn't want to bring a springer into a household in which normally caged birds are occasionally allowed loose, either. Just remember the dog's heritage. Brownie's own instinct and countless generations of training and selective breeding have embedded in her a desire to catch and silence that fluttering wing.

In Summary

Author and breed judge Maxwell Riddle listed four desirable traits most frequently found in springers—boldness, attention, love, and the capacity to take punishment in stride. He went on to say that boldness means curiosity, explaining that the "shy, uncurious Springer is not truly a Springer Spaniel despite his pedigree." Riddle also tells us, that because a springer can give you its full attention, it can concentrate on learning its lessons. He tells us that a springer's capacity for love turns it into the "biggest, strongest, toughest lapdog of all." Finally, he praises its natural endurance in the presence of briers, sleet, or icy water that makes hunting with a springer a pleasure.

Another springer lover, summing up a heated discussion with two friends dedicated to Irish setters and Labrador retrievers, said, "What you have to understand is, my springer doesn't stop to point at the bird, he takes off running and grabs hold of it. And he can keep up with any Lab in the water and swim circles around some of them. At home, he loves my kids, and he barks when friend or foe comes up to the gate. What more do you want of a dog? Maybe other dogs can do one or two things better, but for an all-around companion, I wouldn't trade my English springer spaniel for any other breed."

Your New Puppy

The decision to adopt a puppy is not made without thoughtful consideration. Puppies disrupt our daily routines: We can no longer just get up and go. Puppies take a lot of our time. Somebody has to feed a puppy and to clean up after it. Puppies chew on things, litter the yard, scratch doors. Training a puppy involves somebody doing some research and then having some time to put that research into effect. Puppies are expensive. After the initial purchase, food, veterinarians, and fencing add an additional cost. Why would anyone ever go to the trouble of housetraining a noisy, litterbug of a puppy?

Obviously for some people, the negative aspects of dog ownership are far outweighed by the positive ones. Puppies are loving, adventuresome, tireless creatures. Puppies are responsive, inquisitive beings capable of experiencing and offering happiness, pride, and satisfaction. Puppies mature into loyal canine companions that sit at our side as we work our own way through life, seeming to share our joys and sorrows.

That's why we put up with puppies, to enjoy the friendship of an animal that thinks we're great.

And the feeling is mutual. One study estimated that at least one million dogs have been named beneficiaries in wills. In reflection, writer Christopher Morley wrote, "No one appreciates the very special genius of your conversation as a dog does."

The Purchase Decision

It seems that one merely has to voice a wish for a dog and somebody knows somebody who has a new litter. "They're pretty little puppies," they'll say. "No problem."

All puppies are "pretty little puppies." How can one be sure, once the decision has been made, that you and that puppy will like each other once the newness has worn off?

Purebred or Mixed Breed?

There is nothing wrong with getting a mixed-breed dog. Mixed breeds (nicknamed "Heinz 57" in reference to a famous catsup company) can be loving, even-tempered pets. Mixed-breed dogs have been part of our life from the beginning. After all, historically, new breeds are those "mixed" from established ones. Perhaps you can find stable, well-cared-for, mixed-breed puppies in your neighbor's backyard. The local shelter usually identifies as closely as possible, mixed breeds up for adoption. Read your local newspaper. Chances are, you'll find a classified ad offering puppies from stray matches "free to a good home."

The problem with owning a mixed-breed dog is that we often know little about the puppy's parents, its health care, its potential abilities, or its socialization. Even so, these dogs are often intelligent, healthy, and make wonderful pets. If you do decide to adopt a mixed-breed dog, examine the dog closely. Try to identify its most dominant hereditary traits. Inquire about its parents. Ask a veterinarian to help you. Then read a book about the breed that seems closest to your pet. Much of the information on inheritable traits and the training suggestions will be valuable.

The principal benefit to owning a purebred dog is that one can predict the dog's future physical, social, and temperamental traits with some accuracy. When we hear that a purebred dog is "registered," with one of the major kennel clubs, for instance, we know that for a number of generations that dog's ancestors have been of the identical breed. We can learn a lot more than breed lineage from a dog's registration papers, and we will cover that subsequently (see page 39). For the moment, we can presume that a registered dog, for which we have the papers, is of a certain "pure" breed. (If a dog is said to be purebred but it does not have papers it may or may not be purebred. Without papers there is no proof that the line is unbroken.)

The American Kennel Club recognizes 136 dog breeds, divided into seven groups categorized by type. This allows a wide range of choices to prospective dog owners. For example, if you want a small lapdog you might want to consider a pet from among the seventeen breeds of Group 5, toys. (Eight of the spaniels are toys; the remainder are classified as Group 1, sporting dogs.)

In summary, choosing a purebred dog gives the owner a better chance of owning a pet that matches his or her own standards and preferences.

Kennels, Private Breeders

The major kennels advertise nationally in the classified section of magazines devoted to dogs. Selecting a dog from a popular kennel often involves a delay of several months, perhaps because there is a waiting list, or because the right mating cannot be scheduled until a later time. Particularly if one plans to show or to field-train a dog, a puppy from a line of proven champions can be an excellent investment.

Private breeders usually advertise locally or within a limited area. These so-called backyard breeders seem to be of two kinds. Family Number 1 has an even-tempered family dog, a registered female. This female is mated to a registered male, usually a local stud. Little thought is given to bloodlines, heredity, or faults. When the puppies arrive, they will be adorable. They will be thoroughly and lovingly tended to, and at seven weeks or so, sold as a result of classified advertising. This family may or may not raise another litter. Their puppies typically will not be outstanding in any way except as good family dogs.

Family 2 has a family dog that they show in conformation. The family is aware of breed problems and has had their female tested for hip dysplasia, eye entropion, canine brucellosis, and parasites. Through their breed clubs and show contacts the family searches for the right stud exhibiting the particular physical and temperamental characteristics that they desire. Family 2 may require prospective purchasers to have a fenced in area, among other considerations, often rejecting buyers who don't conform to their standards. The family cares about the welfare of their puppies for life, offering health guarantees. Most will take back one of their puppies if a problem develops or the new owners can no longer care for it. Their puppies typically will be good family dogs. Some may have championship qualities.

Pet Shops

Particularly in the spring, when the puppies arrive, mall pet shops are a primary source of entertainment for the children who gaze longingly through windowed crates at winsome puppies gazing longingly back at them. Here at the shop, more than anywhere else, children have a chance to view the dog kingdom's most admired breeds. Rare and wonderful "monkey dogs," bristly, wrinkled Shar-pei puppies, and handsomely spotted dalmatians attract everyone. Many succumb to the desire to carry home that ball of fur, to release it from its crate and set it free.

What is lacking is the informed purchase decision. When a decision is made merely on the basis of a set of soulful eyes, one needs to remember that all puppies are soulful and appealingly cuddly. Not even all purebred puppies, however, receive the same standard of care.

"Puppy mills," those kennels operated by breeders who mass produce popular breeds, often sell under-socialized puppies weaned too early. Some of these mass-production operations breed their females every season and at the very least keep poor records. In the event that one of these kennel lines develops a genetic or basic health problem the breeders are too far away from the point of sale to be aware of it. Such puppies often can be identified by a certain listlessness and lack of sparkle usually associated with a quality puppy. Avoid those that appear stressed or unusually highstrung.

Most pet shop attendants, aware of the public dismay with these operations, try to be knowledgeable about their puppies' former homes and to buy puppies from steady, reliable suppliers that are often well-known, responsible breeders. Although many breed clubs advise their members not to sell to pet shops, these shops can be a source of good quality dogs and accurate advice on feeding and health care procedures. Aware of the importance of socialization, the shop employees frequently cuddle and play with their puppies, often allowing potential owners that pleasure, also.

If you have made a decision to purchase a particular breed, and that breed is available in a pet shop, the clerk should be happy to tell you about the puppy's background and its parents, perhaps showing you a family photograph or two as well. Certainly many fine tools for feeding, training, and exercising puppies are available at the well-stocked shop.

Shelters, Rescued Dogs

Unfortunately, all too many puppies grow up in busy families who have no time to properly train their little newcomer. These puppies reach adolescence having only learned that loneliness can be cured by wailing, that teething aches can be eased by chewing whatever is handy, and, worst of all, that people can be intimidated by snarling and snapping. These puppies grow up to become misfits through no fault of their own. Their families, according to inclination, take the throw-away dog for a car ride, dropping it off at the nearest crossroads, or head for the nearest animal shelter.

When young and obviously untrained dogs are dropped off at the shelter, those dedicated workers assess the dog. Is it healthy? Has it been mistreated? Is it purebred? Is it aggressive? Would the dog, if trained, make a good family pet?

The staff tries very hard to place the dog with another family. In their effort to reduce the number of free-roaming pets, many shelters require that the dog be spayed or neutered before placing it for adoption. If the dog is too young for the procedure, payment is taken in advance and a temporary certificate is issued. Dogs that can't be placed fall into the statistical six million dogs a year destroyed in shelters.

Shelters often work with local breed clubs, or with rescue leagues such as the Eastern English Springer Spaniel Rescue, Inc., in Dunstable, Massachusetts, that finds homes for abandoned, unwanted, or victimized springers.

Age, Sex, Temperament

Few can resist the appeal of a puppy. The charm of a young animal overpowers the resistance of the most reluctant. The responsibility of feeding, training, and caring for a youngster is often the last consideration for the smitten. Those who do have the time and inclination to raise a puppy are rewarded by the sure pleasure of watching a young animal grow and develop into a well-trained, handsome adult.

Let us not forget, however, the older dog that often, through no fault of its own, loses its home and goes back on the market. People move, retire, travel, lose their jobs, enter nursing homes, all reasons for not being able to care for a dog. They search among their family and acquaintances for someone to take over the dog's care. When all else fails, these families take their pets, ideal candidates for adoption, to the local shelter.

Occasionally, aggressive adolescent dogs, from 9 to 13 months of age, that have not received the proper training, are brought to shelters. Strong, confident owners, with the assistance of a professional trainer, can redeem these wayward juveniles, transforming them into the canine good citizens they are capable of becoming.

Your New Puppy

The question is often asked: Are male or female dogs better as pets? The answer is complicated. Both sexes can be equally well trained and equally affectionate. Female springers come into heat at least once a year and must be confined. Males often roam the neighborhood and beyond in instinctive response to that distracting lure of a female in heat. Both of these potential problems can be handled by the owner. The female can be spayed, and the male can be neutered, and they often will be better pets for it.

As far as temperament goes, either sex can be aggressive, either can be possessive, either can be boisterous, either can be lazy. Behavior depends partly on heredity, partly on environment and training. With the exception of genetic abnormalities, the eventual temperament of the dog is pretty much up to you.

Pet Personality Test

Every day, students of animal behavior learn a little more about the dog. Moreover, studies of young animals have helped psychologists in their work with children. Behaviorists around the world share information on procedures and techniques designed to help us understand the world's oldest domesticated animal. In 1963, Clarence Pfaffenberger, in an effort to develop guidelines for his work at Guide Dogs for the Blind, published the results of his studies on dog behavior. When the institute began its work with dogs, only 8 percent of the dogs enrolled in the program graduated successfully. Consequently, Pfaffenberger set out first to define the personality traits possessed by successful Guide Dogs, and then to identify those tendencies in puppies. Within a few years, with work, study, and clinical assistance, new statistics emerged. Today, over 90 percent of the puppies selected complete the Guide Dog training. What caused this amazing turnaround, and how can we learn from it?

Dog behavior testing is based on close observation of the puppy at certain ages of its development, and under standardized conditions. Behaviorists have proved, for instance, that there are certain times in its life when a dog can do its best learning. Puppies, for instance, cannot be taught anything before they are 21 days old. From 21 to 49 days (three to seven weeks), however, a puppy will do its best learning, either with your help, or by itself. The secret is, to be present during those periods when the puppy can best accept guidance.

In 1975, William Campbell, whose work with problem dogs is well known, suggested five tests that would reveal future behavioral tendencies. If properly carried out, when the puppies are about seven weeks old, tests such as these help to match dog and owner compatibilities.

The puppy's confidence, or social attraction as Campbell terms it, is measured by how readily and happily a strange pup will come to you. Place the puppy in the center of an area and step away from it. Kneel down and gently clap your hands. How quickly the pup comes, or whether it comes at all, are both reflections of its social independence.

Next, see if the puppy will follow you. Walk away from it in a normal manner and do not call to it. Be sure it sees you walk away. Failure to follow, or lack of interest reveals the puppy's degree of following attraction.

Will the puppy accept restraint? Turn the puppy over, belly up. With one hand, hold the puppy down for thirty seconds. Does it lie submissively? Does it struggle for awhile and then lie submissively? How hard does it struggle? Do you want a more dominant or a more submissive pet?

Top left: The springer: a people dog if ever the name was deserved.
Top right: The companionship of a friend on a long morning walk is a pleasure not to be forgotten.
Bottom left: It's not too early to learn the basic commands.
Bottom: right: An experienced partnership showing off their training under the judge's watchful eye.

Can you stroke the puppy from head to tail without it jumping up, growling or nipping at you? Does it just walk away from you? Does it accept this stroking, which is a sign of social dominance on your part?

With both hands pick up the puppy and hold it just off the ground for at least thirty seconds. You are now in total control. How well does the puppy accept elevation dominance? Does it wiggle, nip, or wait patiently?

Campbell tells us that an extremely dominant dog, one that scores high in all categories is a poor choice for families with small children, or for elderly people. If properly trained and if part of a calm, adult household, these dogs make wonderful pets.

Conversely, a dog that shows a high degree of submission must also be in the proper household. Although these dogs have few aggressive tendencies, their low level of confidence will require plenty of praise during training, and thoughtful handling to bring out their latent confidence.

These preceding tests indicate the importance of observing a dog carefully before you bring it home. Each breed has tendencies, but each dog is an individual. These guidelines, and your breeder's help can provide a basis for your decision. Most breeders today use a combination of some kind of testing and personal, up-close evaluation and can be of tremendous help to you when making your selection.

Bringing Your Pet Home

Before the big day arrives, a thoughtful owner will have on hand a few basic puppy necessities

Top left: The water-loving springer enjoys games.
Top right: Add the companionship of a second springer and the games are limitless.
Middle left: Who's winning.
Middle right: Race you to the buoy.
Bottom left: I touched base first.
Bottom right: Let's do it again.

such as food and a bowl to put it in, a water dish, and a comfortable bed. Later the puppy will need a brush, a collar and leash, and perhaps a toy or two.

Bring your puppy home when someone, preferably the primary caregiver, has two or three days to spend with it. The puppy will be lonesome for its littermates. It will miss the warmth and sleeping companionship of a box full of puppies. It is up to you, its new owner, to make it feel welcome and at home.

A Place of Its Own

As a new member of your family, your puppy will appreciate knowing the rules. It is best to make some thoughtful decisions even before the puppy arrives, and it is very important to be consistent when applying those rules. Basic considerations regarding where the puppy will sleep, where it will eliminate, who will feed it, and who will train it must be addressed ahead of time.

When you arrive home, take the puppy right away to the place you have selected for it to eliminate. Wait while it does its business, which shouldn't be long coming. Praise the puppy, play with the puppy, scoop it up in your arms, and take it into the house.

The puppy's bed should be located in a quiet corner away from the house traffic patterns but near the family's activity center. It will want to be a part of any function to the point that it will risk getting stepped on to participate.

Unless you intend to crate-train your puppy, it is not necessary to purchase a special bed for the puppy's use. Wicker baskets are pretty, but a young spaniel can be quite destructive. It is better to begin with a soft nest of towels and a cardboard box for awhile. Later you can upgrade when necessary. Cut out a small door in the box, turn it upside down, and allow the puppy to crawl inside. Your puppy will feel safe in this makeshift cave and spend many hours in it. If you do intend to crate-train your puppy, and we suggest that the long-term benefits are of great value to both of you, suggestions follow.

Your New Puppy

The Crate as Hearth and Home

The purpose of a crate is to simulate a den. Don't be misled by the comparison of a crated puppy to a caged zoo animal deprived of any freedom. Pay no attention to those who commiserate with the puppy on its confinement. Enjoy instead, the knowledge that you have selected a proven aid to puppy rearing. Used properly, crating works for both worlds. You will soon realize that your puppy enjoys its crate, indeed will return to it voluntarily seeing in it a secure haven, a place it can hide when overwhelmed by stomping, threatening feet. A crate is a quiet place where a puppy can nap without worry knowing its family is nearby. You yourself will learn to appreciate the crate as a housetraining tool of enormous importance.

The Right Toys

Puppies are playful animals chasing leaves, squirrels, and birds with equal joy. We enjoy watching our puppies at play and often join them at their games, providing them with balls and specially made chew toys. Puppies with freedom to run in the yard don't need many special toys, however, as long as they have an assortment of sticks, leaves, and pine cones to play with. A puppy soon selects a favorite stick, for instance, carries it around for hours, sets it down, and loses it. Some time later, occasionally days later, the stick will reappear; the puppy will carry it proudly, gnaw it for awhile, and again abandon it for a squirrel chase.

We should be cautious about giving a puppy lightweight plastic toys that shred easily. Puppies have been known to tear off and swallow whistles, noisemakers, and button-eyes from furry toys. Some authorities recommend offering the puppy an old leather glove to chew on. It has your smell and you probably misplaced the mate, anyhow. Do try to avoid giving your puppy an old shoe, however. While you are unlikely to leave your new gloves lying around, your shoes are often on the floor. Your puppy cannot distinguish between a shoe you will permit it to chew on and a new pair of shoes.

We provided our family's puppies with chew hooves which were instant favorites, an assortment of hard vinyl bones which we removed before they splintered, and homemade toys such as knotted white cotton socks. One favorite trick is to tie a sock around a canning jar ring. The combination has a satisfactory carry-handle and makes a wonderful clanking noise when dragged on the floor.

Not by the Ears

One U.S. president received a lot of attention from the press when he was photographed lifting his pet beagles by the ears. Although the beagles didn't howl, animal lovers did. You wouldn't pick your springer up by those marvelous ears, but we can hurt our puppies in other ways by not following the correct lifting procedures.

Puppies are wiggly, unwieldy fur balls. Some puppies resent being lifted off the floor. Some are frightened. When the puppies squirm trying to free themselves, they may be dropped.

The proper way to lift a puppy is to use two hands. Place one hand under the puppy's heavy little bottom and place the other hand on the puppy's chest between the front legs. The puppy is almost in a sitting position. Don't let anyone grab the puppy around the stomach to lift it; don't let anyone lift the puppy by the scruff of the neck and please, not by the ears.

Housetraining Your Puppy

Dogs are naturally clean animals. That statement may sound funny at first, especially if you have ever had to clean up a floor or a carpet after a pet has had an "accident" on it. Observe the mother of a litter as she demonstrates the truth of that belief, however.

Your New Puppy

When the puppies are born, the mother cleans them up and eats the afterbirth. She frequently licks, massages, and turns her puppies thus forcing them to move, breathe, and eliminate. So powerful is the force driving her that for two weeks she rarely leaves the puppies, but perseveres with her licking and massaging them, forcing them to eliminate and disposing of the waste.

At about 3 weeks of age, however, the puppies are somewhat ambulatory. The mother's natural instinct for cleanliness, enforced by a sharp nip if necessary, convinces the puppies to eliminate some distance away from the central gathering place. The accepted distance gets progressively farther until even the laziest puppy is motivated to eliminate outside the nest.

Animal behaviorists tell us that we can take advantage of this learned puppy behavior of not soiling its own bed by adapting this early training to the puppy's new environment.

The following are suggestions that have worked for others. It is very hard to generalize because your springer puppy is not like any other springer puppy. Your puppy may not be 7 weeks of age, the ideal adoption period. Your puppy may handle stress differently than other puppies. Moreover, you may be very experienced and need no assistance in raising puppies. But for the first-time puppy owner, the suggestions that follow will help. By understanding what is happening between you and the puppy, these suggestions can be modified and personalized to fit your needs.

Be consistent: Feed the puppy at the same times every day. Take it to the same place outside every time it needs to eliminate. Take the puppy in and out the same door. And stay with the puppy. If you put the puppy out and go back inside it will likely wait on the steps until you let it back in and then finish its business in the house.

Be enthusiastic: Praise the puppy. Cuddle it. Talk to it. Laugh with it. Play with it. Make that puppy want to please you more than anything else

Teach children not to lift the puppy by its front legs, its stomach, and certainly not by its ears.

in life. Be sure it knows when you are pleased. Stroke it. Nuzzle it. Be a friend.

Be observant: Take advantage of the puppy's natural instincts. Watch for signs of discomfort. Even a very young puppy (6 or 7 weeks old) when confined to a crate, will bark and whine when it has to eliminate. It will do its best to avoid soiling its bed.

Although even a very young puppy's bladder can be contained for six or seven hours at night, in daytime it must eliminate after every nap, every meal and every play session. It may seem like you're on call every two or three hours all day. Nevertheless, train yourself in the daytime to respond to the early signals. Watch for sniffing along the floor or walking in circles, both obvious signs that the search is on.

Be smart: Don't let the puppy get overstimulated. As soon as everyone has greeted and petted the puppy, reclaim it. Put the puppy in its crate for about ten minutes. Speak softly to it, and go about your business, keeping within its hearing range. The puppy should fall asleep. If, despite your best efforts, the puppy is still awake and is whimpering, take it out, cuddle it, talk to it, and then put it back in the crate for another ten minutes or so.

Crate Training

Those owners who elect to crate-train their puppies will receive quicker response and will be more pleased with learning retention than those using other methods. The concept behind crate training is to replace the den image embedded in the animal's brain. A den represents to an animal the security from predators and comfort from the elements that it instinctively seeks. For lucky pets and their owners, crates are not just a method of housetraining but a way of life.

Crates, available from pet supply stores and from catalogs, are made in many sizes and of several materials. Collapsible metal or fiberglass crates tend to be the most popular. For economy's sake select a crate that will accommodate a full grown springer, at least 3 feet (.9 m) square. (A larger size will not bother the puppy). Because you can expect your springer to stand approximately 26 to 27 inches (65–67 cm) tall, its crate should be no less than 30 inches (75 cm) high.

Happily at home, puppy relaxes in its own private den.

Have the crate on hand before you bring the puppy home. Don't try to set up a crate for the very young puppy in the garage or in a room shut off from the family. It will be profoundly unhappy. Set it up in a location from which the puppy can see the family activity, yet one that will be out of the main traffic flow. A corner of the kitchen or family room is fine. Inside the crate, place a washable mat or rug for the puppy to lie down on. If you like, you may include a chew toy, but this is not necessary at the outset. Do not put any food or water in the crate.

Set up a feeding station at one particular place and always feed the puppy there. Decide on a convenient feeding schedule according to its age and adhere to it strictly. Provide an outdoor elimination spot and take the puppy frequently.

Lengthen crate time gradually. Even at 16 weeks of age, two hours is the maximum crate time for a puppy unless it is deeply asleep. Keep an ear open for sounds. Although puppies do sleep a lot, they periodically awaken to eliminate and search for food, water, and attention.

Paper Training

Teaching your puppy to eliminate outdoors is the best way to reduce messy accidents in the house. Some family situations, however, such as bad weather, apartment living, or work routines, lend themselves more conveniently to paper training.

The basic theory behind paper training is to teach the puppy to eliminate on the newspaper and only on the newspaper. Because puppies instinctively seek out a spot that has been used before your task is to select that spot before the puppy does, and to remind the puppy of its location.

Your puppy will have poor marksmanship in the beginning, therefore you must cover a fairly wide area with paper. A thick layer, double-page size is usually sufficient.

Your New Puppy

The procedure is the same as for outside. Take the puppy to its spot and wait with it until the deed has been performed. Praise the puppy when it has completed the job. Take the puppy out of the room. Then, later, remove the soiled sheets, leaving behind the bottom sheets that will still retain the odors. Place these bottom sheets on top of the next stack of papers, and so on.

Cleaning Up After Your Pet

Accidents will happen. If you see the puppy dribbling, pick it up immediately, saying "No!" in a very firm voice and carry it, still dribbling if necessary, to its elimination spot. Because puppies are creatures of habit, and because they return to the "scene of the crime," douse the spot with an odor eliminator. Several chemical solutions are on the market and all work well if applied immediately. The combination of bacteria and enzyme in some removes the odor and actually "eats" the organic matter.

If you do not have access to or do not wish to use one of the enzyme products, we can suggest several homemade remedies. Two that are proven to work are ordinary powdered cornstarch or a solution of diluted vinegar. Whatever product you select, the procedure described next is essentially the same for all.

If the accident is on a carpet, blot as much moisture as you can with an old towel or several layers of paper toweling. Press down with your foot in order remove as much moisture as possible from the padding. If you are using an enzyme, follow the manufacturer's directions. If you decide to use cornstarch, dry the spot as much as possible and then layer on a generous amount. Cover the spot and let dry. Vacuum later. The cornstarch will have absorbed the moisture and the odor.

The vinegar treatment requires that the rug be colorfast. Test it on an inconspicuous corner first to be sure. Then, mix one part of vinegar to two

With patience, both puppy and family will agree on the proper elimination procedure.

parts of water. Pour onto the spot approximately as much vinegar as there was urine. Allow the solution to sit for five minutes. Again, blot all the moisture with a towel or paper toweling. Weigh down and let dry. The odor should be gone.

Notes: First, never use a product containing ammonia to clean up a urine odor. It is the ammonia in the urine that we are trying to remove. Second, perform the cleanup activity after the puppy is out of the room. And third, keep the puppy away from the spot at least overnight.

Learning to Stay Alone

Your puppy is a social animal. It grew up in a litter. It will not want to stay alone. Bereft of its mother and littermates, it will set up a lonesome wail for company. Although this part of puppy training is sometimes the hardest, and a few sleepless hours are to be expected, those who have been there before us have left a few helpful suggestions to help us make it through.

Your New Puppy

The First Nights

It is your puppy. It will be your forty- or fifty-pound dog. If you don't mind your springer sleeping in the bedroom with you, bring it in, by all means. If you do want to train it to sleep alone, be very matter of fact about your wishes.

Be sure the puppy eliminates late in the evening, preferably right before your bedtime. Take it to its bed, cuddle it, give it a chance to settle down, then go out and close the door. Don't go far. Chances are the puppy will demand that you return. Go back in. Talk to the puppy. Reassure it, cuddle it, and leave again.

Here's the hard part. If the puppy continues to wail, the last thing you want to do is to give it the impression that you will return on call. This time, if you are sure it is fed and doesn't have to eliminate, knock sharply on the door and call out "No!" The point is to startle the puppy into seeing a relationship between its fussing and the loud noise. It also gets the idea that its new friend is displeased. The puppy may be so weary that it will curl up and go to sleep until early, very early, the next morning. Consider yourself lucky.

Helpful Hints

Because puppy lovers understand that the puppy longs for companionship, noise, closeness, and warmth, owners have been very inventive in trying to replace in its life whatever will reproduce these conditions. You might find some of the following suggestions helpful.

• Place a ticking clock nearby.
• Tune a radio to an all-night talk station.
• Donate an old, unwashed sweatshirt to the nest.
• Wrap a hot water bottle in a soft towel.
• Provide a favorite chew toy.
• Close your bedroom door.

The Adult Springer

Springer puppies are charming, fun-loving animals bent on exploring every inch of land, tasting every fallen leaf, and turning over every stick in reach. We enjoy watching puppies learn the smells, tastes, and sights of their new world.

The cutest springer puppy, however, is destined to be first a gangly adolescent and then a mature, responsible companion. How does it make the transition? How can you help?

General Care

Unless groomed for a show career, Willie, the family springer that spends most of his time indoors, does not need intensive shaping or trimming. His coat will thin in response to the indoor climate. Springers kept in outdoor kennels all winter, including those that frequently hunt, however, do grow a full, wooly coat and will benefit from some trimming around the toe pads, topknot, and tail each spring.

Provided Willie stays away from mud puddles, skunks, and garbage cans he will rarely require a bath. Generally speaking, a twice weekly brushing with a medium bristle brush should remove matted hair and keep his waterproof coat in good shape. Besides, your dog will love the attention. Willie's pendulous ears, on the other hand, do demand rather more frequent attention than some breeds.

Barring any unusual circumstances, the following schedule should keep your dog clean, healthy, and pest free.

Clipping

The springer's silky coat does require frequent grooming and brushing to remove the sticks, burrs, and stray weed seeds that seem to attach themselves to ears and tails and underbellies. The unbrushed, untrimmed springer soon develops a mat of dead hair that is both unsightly and uncomfortable. An occasional clipping of ear hair and hair between the toes will help your springer feel

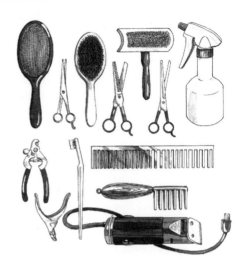

Grooming tools: bristle brushes, wide tooth combs, carders, thinning shears, nail clippers, sprays, and razor.

better. Occasional attention to the topknot and the tip of the tail will help your pet look better, too.

It is important to start early. A very young springer can learn to stand quietly for its trim and to enjoy the massage and attention that follows. Alternatively, dogs not introduced at a young age to the noise of clippers and blow dryers will have a difficult time adjusting to even basic grooming procedures.

Books are available detailing the springer cuts, but the personal advice of a professional is not to be ignored. These groomers provide the experience and attention to detail that many springer owners desire for their pets. Their advice can be indispensable. Dedicated owners—with advice, experience, and patience—can learn to keep their springers in good trim, but an occasional trip to the beauty parlor helps everyone.

Bathing

When the inevitable time comes that Willie will need a bath, you will know it.

The Adult Springer

When you wash your springer, prepare to do a thorough job, taking care of all the odds and ends that somehow get lost these busy days. Old clothes, old towels, a mild commercial dog shampoo, lukewarm water, and plenty of elbow room are prime requisites. Have on hand some cotton to stuff in his ears, some swabs to clean out his ears and eyes, a nail clipper for toenails, and a medium bristle brush.

First, brush the dog thoroughly. Examine it for fleas, ticks, and hot spots (patches of bare skin that weep and cause pain). Look for bruises or unusual lumps or tender places. Check your dog's feet. Trim any unnecessary hair from around its toes. Trim its toenails if necessary.

Begin the actual bath by lathering a ring around the dog's neck. This will prevent any fleas or other critters that are scurrying to escape from the soap from gathering on the dog's face. Move on to the back and stomach. Don't forget to pay special attention to the tail, the toes, and shoulder joints.

The secret to a good wash is a good rinse. Don't leave a soap residue on the dog. Rinse and rinse again. If the day is warm, let Willie run for awhile and shake off the excess water

Check the nails of indoor pets at least once a month.

before towel drying him. In bad weather, towel dry him immediately, and keep him inside at least overnight.

Ears

The springer's ear, like that of its other spaniel cousins, is long and pendulous. When at rest, the ear lies close to the head, a position that blocks air and light from entering and allows moisture to settle within the ear canal. Consequently, ears should be checked at least once a week for wax buildup, parasites, or ear infections. Don't probe into the ear canal itself. Merely keep the inside of the ears clean by swabbing with a moistened cotton swab. If you have done all you can and feel a deeper cleaning is needed, a visit to the veterinarian is in order.

Eyes

Pay special attention to your springer's eyes. Even after a day of traveling through land no more foreign than the brush of your backyard, the weed seeds and biting insects can make a dog's life miserable. If you suspect a problem, call your veterinarian.

Teeth and Nails

Treat Willie's teeth with the same care you give your own. Feeding dry kibble is an excellent way to keep his teeth in shape. A strong Nylabone makes an excellent toothbrush. Although some owners periodically brush their dog's teeth with a toothbrush dipped in a 3 percent hydrogen peroxide solution or a commercial doggie toothpaste, many owners refuse to learn the procedure, leaving that chore to the veterinarian. If you do choose to brush your springer's teeth, start when it is a puppy and accustom it to the sensation at an early age.

No doubt Willie's nails were trimmed by the breeder. Puppy nails seem to grow overnight and will leave marks and picks on the nursing mother unless trimmed. Perhaps your pet does not need a trim. This is likely if it spends a lot of time out of doors or on hard surfaces. The most likely indication that nails need trimming is sound: As one breeder phrased it, "if you hear a click, cut."

Exercising Your Springer

If your springer is a hunter, or a country dog blessed with endless property on which to roam, you may not need to add additional exercise to its daily routine. But if, like many of today's springers, yours is almost housebound, or at least confined to a small backyard, your pet's health and outlook on life will benefit by an exercise program.

Walking, running, chasing, running beside your bicycle, and Frisbee and ball playing are viable forms of exercise that are both companionable and beneficial to your pet. The only warning would be a suggestion to monitor the level of effort expended. Puppies and adolescent dogs can be damaged by overexertion. Your adult springer can probably keep up with you. If you are exercising a puppy, however, stop at once if you see heavy panting or decreased speed.

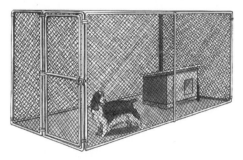

The outdoor run provides a safe place until the family returns home.

This two-room dog house was constructed with comfort in mind.

An Outdoor Run

If Willie is an outdoor pet, you probably already have a doghouse set up in an out of the way location in your backyard, so constructed and situated as to shelter him from winter winds and driving spring rains.

If you haven't constructed the kennel house yet, keep a few points in mind:
- Raise the floor several inches off the ground for additional air circulation in summer. Check for drafts in winter.
- Provide plenty of dry bedding. A chintz dog pillow looks pretty, but if the filling gets wet your dog will get chilled. If you don't want to invest in a waterproof pillow, then clean straw, wood chips, or even shredded paper—changed once a week—make fine beds.
- Willie will lie facing the entrance you use most frequently, so make it easy for him. Position the kennel opening so that he faces the door or the gate you use most frequently.

- If you cannot fence in your entire yard, construct a dog run around the kennel. Runs can be purchased from supply houses or constructed on site of galvanized, 11-gauge, zinc-coated wire. Installing the fence on top of a narrow concrete slab will prevent your pet from digging under the fence. For springers, an 8-by-16-foot (2.4 × 5 m) enclosed exercise run is adequate.
- Set the kennel house up against the garage or another solid structure for added protection from winter winds and rains.
- Willie is an outside dog, but on truly bitter winter nights, if his kennel has no heat, house your pet inside.

Registering Your Springer

Springers traditionally are registered through one of two national organizations, the American Kennel Club or the United Kennel Club. Write them for more information about either organization; their addresses are listed in the Useful Literature and Addresses section (see page 87) of this book.

The American Kennel Club

The American Kennel Club (AKC), established in 1884, maintains a registry listing the ancestral record of each dog on its lists. This record is known as the Stud Book. When a litter is produced as the result of a mating between two registered dogs, the owner of the mother dog (the dam) notifies the AKC by completing and submitting a litter application. This application is ordinarily mailed off within a few weeks of birth, certainly no later than six weeks afterward. The AKC responds by returning to the owner one certificate for each puppy. This certificate, known as the blue form, is then turned over to the new owners. It is this blue form that the final owner sends back to the AKC (along with the appropriate fee), to request an AKC Registration Certificate.

The United Kennel Club

The United Kennel Club (UKC), founded in 1898, is primarily a working dog registry. The UKC also maintains a registration service, and encourages a "total dog" philosophy among its members: Handlers and breeders are encouraged to retain the natural hunting or working instincts of the dog. Breeding strictly for conformation (the show ring) is discouraged. The UKC proudly states that "the majority of the dogs we register still perform the tasks the breeds were originally bred for."

Why Bother with Registration at All?

The somewhat cumbersome routine of registration has one primary purpose: to certify purebred dogs. Each purebred springer puppy has its own unique identification number that will follow it through life. That registration shows that all its ancestors were springers. It shows which ancestors received which titles and certifies that it possessed certain championship qualities it may have passed on to its offspring.

Limited Registration

Many responsible dog owners agree that too many unwanted dogs are dropped off on country roads, taken to animal shelters, or abandoned to roam streets and neighborhoods in search of food, shelter, and companionship. Unfortunately, thousands of dogs are euthanized each year.

In their effort to control the breeding of pet dogs, many breeders today sell pet quality puppies with a written spay/neuter agreement. The registration papers are withheld until proof of the surgery is received.

Even though the spay/neuter agreement could be rescinded by the breeder, many—believing that some puppies are "late bloomers"—hesitated to force such a final decision on their puppies. In January 1990, these breeders, seeking an alternative to the spay/neuter contract, established an AKC procedure for limited registration of litters. Although these puppies themselves are recognized as pure-bred dogs their offspring cannot be registered.

This is not to be confused with the 1991 UKC Limited Privilege Registration Program. In a commendable effort to allow non-purebred dogs to participate in their obedience programs, the UKC offers what it calls single-registration privileges. These dogs must be phenotypically recognizable (that is, they should look like a beagle, for instance, or look like a springer) and must be spayed or neutered.

Pedigrees

A pedigree is a written record of Willie's ancestry as recorded in the registration books. We can learn a great deal about our dogs by studying their pedigrees. Even a four-generation pedigree, for instance, contains the full names, birthdates, and titles earned of 30 dogs in your pet's family tree.

How to Read a Pedigree: The term pedigree comes from the French *pied de grue* or "Crane's foot." Apparently, long ago, some inspired researcher decided that the lineage lines of a genealogy chart resembled the spread foot of a crane. As with any effort worth pursuing, it takes some inspiration and a great deal of backup information to follow through on today's pedigrees. But from a full four-generation pedigree, the patient inquirer can obtain a great deal of knowledge about a puppy's possibilities.

On the top lines a pedigree lists your dog's name, its breed, sex, color, birthdate, and the name of the breeder. The Registration number (a six-digit number with a two-letter prefix) is a source of lifetime identification.

In the body of an AKC certified pedigree, for instance, the four-generation certificate will list similar information for your puppy's parents through their great-great grandparents. Also listed will be their ancestors' registration numbers, dates of registration, coat color, if requested, and any

AKC titles earned. By reading carefully with access to a good breed book, you can determine your dog's most likely good and not-so-good traits. Imagine finding out that one of the top Field Trial winners of all time is in your dog's pedigree! Or maybe you'll find Millie, who was the White House springer during the Bush administration!

Traveling with Your Springer

Willie hates to be left at home, and, much preferring to accompany his family on outings, never asks where the car is going, just when. These outings can turn into unpleasant memories unless the dog is well behaved.

Car Rides

Begin Willie's training in car courtesy by taking him on short, fun rides. Insist that he occupy the back seat of the car. Never let Willie ride with his head sticking out the window. A flying bug hitting his cornea will cause a lot of pain and possibly cause permanent damage to his sight.

Because dogs are less and less welcome in our public lives, our pets must occasionally be left unattended in a parked car. In warm weather, if you must leave your dog in the car while you run in for a brief errand, try to park beneath a shade tree. Roll a window down. A car can turn into an oven in a very, very short time. Be sure your errand is indeed brief. Not sure about it? Put yourself in your dog's place. Pretend you've been left in the car "just for a minute" and someone else is running in "for a minute." Would you be comfortable in the car? Remember that image next time you decide to leave your dog alone.

On Vacation

Depending on how well a dog is trained, it can be pleasant company on a long trip. If you are

The Adult Springer

Be a good neighbor. On a walk, scoops and plastic baggies are as important as a leash.

leaving on vacation and you are sure Willie will be welcome at your destination, by all means bring him along with you. You might want to pack his own food (sometimes the brands you use at home can be difficult to find elsewhere and this is no time to experiment). Be sure his rabies tags are in place and up to date. Be sure your name, home address, and telephone number, or your veterinarian's telephone number, are on his collar.

Some motels and resorts will accept pets in the room, some have kennel provisions. Check with your travel agent or call before you leave.

If you are traveling in a camper, or tenting, remember that few state or national parks and even fewer private parks allow unleashed pets, so bring a long tie-line for those ocasions.

Airline travel with a dog is not complicated, particularly if no plane change is involved, provided that you make your reservations well in advance. Consult your reservation agent for specific travel requirements.

Boarding Your Springer

For some owners, a vacation with a dog is out of the question. Even though European laws are less strict than our own (dogs are often welcome in parks, plazas, restaurants, hotels, even at the market) their quarantine laws are not. Your pet could be required to spend weeks at the port of entry waiting for a permit.

For these occasions and other times that are unsuitable, a boarding kennel is a haven. Often part of your veterinarian's services, the kennel is staffed by knowledgeable dog lovers, often the same staff that greets Willie during routine visits. Provide a few favorite toys and leave on vacation content that you have made the right decision.

Feeding Your Springer

Ask around and you will discover there are as many different ideas about what to feed a dog as there are products on the shelf.

"Every evening after supper, our dogs, Blondie and Blaze, get a pan of dried dog food mixed with crumbled bread and whatever bones and kitchen scraps I have on hand," one neighbor tells us. "Both dogs are healthy and happy; I'm happy, too, because I don't have any leftovers."

"I buy whatever brand I have a coupon for, or whatever brand is on sale that month," says another neighbor. "I refill a self-feeder twice a week and Rusty eats as much as he wants. He gets plenty of exercise, he's not fat, and this method is a time- and money-saver for me."

The lady from down the street replied, "I buy Duke's food from my vet. We taught him not to beg for snacks, and he doesn't miss them because he's never had them. Yes, it is an expensive diet, but he's worth it."

The neighborhood retiree, queried while walking his pampered pooch, tells us, "My little Magic would rather starve than eat dry dog food. She doesn't even like canned food much, so she eats what we do. I do give her a daily vitamin, though."

Which neighbor is right? Which one is taking better care of a pet? Whom should you believe? What is a new owner to do?

Understanding Canine Nutrition

Each of the neighbors in the story above believes that he or she understands pet nutrition, and each has given some thought to proper feeding. In the light of so many opinions, who can tell which dog owner has the right approach?

Each owner has attempted to provide the necessary nutritional elements while allowing for individual differences and needs on both sides. A little thought coupled with a quick reading of some of the following information should help you to make up your own mind.

We don't have to be nutritionists to feed Tootsie properly. We do, however, need a basic understanding of her needs.

The Basic Elements

The various state departments of agriculture under the Association of American Feed Control Officials (AAFCO) have established national regulations regarding pet food quality that are required of all pet food manufacturers. In addition, the Pet Food Institute, at the behest of veterinarians, recently initiated a Nutrition Assurance Program that uses, among other tests, live animal feeding to monitor manufacturer's claims. The result is that if a manufacturer's label, for instance, states that a food is "complete and balanced," and indicates that AAFCO protocols and procedures were followed, you may be sure that the product has been tested and has passed. So, look for the label. If you do feed an AAFCO tested product, be cautious about adding large amounts of kitchen leftovers to your dog's diet. In particular, do not add any vitamin or mineral supplements unless under the supervision of your veterinarian, as an imbalance could result.

Leading the daily recommendations for a balanced diet are top quality proteins, carbohydrates, fats, vitamins, minerals, and fresh water, in proper proportion.

Proper proportion depends on Tootsie's age, her activity level, her health, and such temporary situations as, for instance, whether she is pregnant or nursing. Tootsie is a big springer, weighing about 50 pounds. As a puppy she required large amounts of carbohydrates and protein. As an active adult she needs less protein, but about half of her calories should still come from carbohydrates. As Tootsie ages we'll reduce the amount of protein even further to help her avoid kidney problems.

These issues are addressed by today's commercial food providers. Once you have decided on a brand, follow the manufacturer's instructions as to age and formula requirements. You and Tootsie will be glad you did.

Types of Dog Food

It really is a matter of personal preference (yours and Tootsie's) and a matter of economics (yours) as to which type of food you feed her as long as that choice contains the proper nutritional levels. The following information may help you reach a decision on feeding.

Canned Food

Canned dog food is cooked, sterile, and convenient. If the label states that the food is nutritionally balanced, such a diet will provide all the necessary nutrients for your pet. About 50 percent of the protein in canned products comes from meat, poultry, or fish products. The remaining protein usually is derived from eggs or dried milk. Dried skim milk and dried buttermilk are common additions. One can of food contains about 450 calories with the carbohydrates provided by corn, barley, or wheat.

Many owners, when comparing packaged and dry dog food with the more costly canned food, find that the latter smells more appealing and looks more realistic than the first two. Although aware that they are paying a premium price for the can's water content, many owners—particularly of smaller breeds—feed canned food exclusively. Economically, this option often is not available to owners of medium or large breeds.

Semimoist Food

The semimoist dog foods, usually wrapped in cellophane packages, contain half the water of canned food. Because they need no refrigeration, even when opened, semimoist packages are con-

venient for travelers or vacationers. If you do plan to use these products as a convenience when traveling, be aware that a sudden change in diet can upset your dog's digestive system. It is best to introduce the change gradually while on home grounds.

A 6-ounce (170 g) pouch or patty contains the equivalent calorie count to a 1-pound (454 g) can of dog food. Although these packaged foods may look like burgers, they are, unlike canned products, relatively odorless, and thus may be unappetizing.

Dry Food

Bagged, loose-pack dry foods are usually granulated, pelleted or flaked, then homogenized and cooked. Each flake or pellet contains a mix of meat meals, grain, and vegetable products. Depending on the brand, certain vitamin and mineral supplements are added to bring the product up to AAFCO standards.

Interestingly, many dry dog foods, even supermarket brands, contain more protein than do canned or semimoist dog foods, and remember that from 20 to 30 percent of your dog's diet should be protein. The chart below is the result of one afternoon's browsing down the pet food aisle of a local market.

Homemade Food

Although AAFCO-approved commercial dog foods guarantee a balanced diet, many pet owners consider, at one time or another, homemade feed-

Canned Brand X	9% Protein
Canned Brand Y	8% Protein
Semimoist Brand A	18% Protein
Dry Brand B	26% Protein
Dry Brand C	21% Protein

ing. Owners of kitchen-raised litters, or orphaned puppies, for instance, often provide special diets for the newcomers.

It is important that the homemade diet follow the proper nutritional guidelines as closely as possible. For puppies, that balance should be close to 25 percent protein, 25 percent fat and 50 percent carbohydrates. Cooked or dry cereal, cooked rice or toast, and cooked hamburger are good starter possibilities. Milk, meat broth, or warm water can be added as necessary. Vegetable oil and vitamin and mineral supplements also can be added as necessary.

Additives and Supplements

Your pet requires vitamins A, D, E, and K as well as vitamin B, niacin, and folic acid just as we do. (Vitamin C is not a recognized dietary requirement for dogs.) Commercial foods labeled as complete or balanced supply adequate amounts of these supplements.

Remember to be careful with dietary supplements. Even adding vitamins and minerals to an already balanced diet can result in serious nutritional deficiencies. Other problems can be caused by erroneous assumptions about a dog's needs. Meat, for instance, is an important part of Tootsie's diet, but an all-meat diet is not nutritionally balanced.

The most important supplement you can give your pet is fresh water. Water is required for all normal cell functions. Because water is not stored in the body but is excreted, a ready supply of fresh water should be available at all times.

Bones and Biscuits

Baked dog bones and biscuits are made by mixing wheat or soybean flour with meat meal, milk products, and vitamin and mineral supplements. The resulting dough is cut into shapes and baked.

Dogs love these starchy treats. They make handy snacks and even handier training helpers. If your pet is overweight, remember to count calories when assessing its diet. Each bone in a nationally advertised, standard size "flavor snack," for instance, contains about 20 calories.

Same Time, Same Place

Dogs appreciate consistency. Because mealtime is often the highlight of Tootsie's day, it would make sense to feed her a fixed, stable diet on a regular schedule.

Some owners successfully introduce a self-feeding schedule that allows the dog to eat from a dispenser-type container filled with dry dog food. Tootsie can consume as much or as little as she likes. Proponents of self-feeding note several advantages.
• Primarily the dog does not have to wait for its supper if its family is late returning from work.
• A dog that nibbles throughout the day maintains a constant level of nutrients in its body.
• Constant nibbling reduces that before-meal time excitement that can cause digestive upsets.

Begging and Other Bad Habits

Begging is cute when it is part of a repertoire of tricks, but begging at the dinner table is not socially acceptable. Trying to teach a frisky springer to beg only when family is present is more than most springers can comprehend. Better not to start the habit at all. The Monks of New Skete, widely praised for their dog training methods, allow their dogs to accompany them to the dining hall. Each animal lies quietly until its master is finished, not leaving its place until given a command.

Finicky Eaters

Most dog behaviorists believe that dogs are trained by us to be picky about the foods they eat. Remember the puppy rule that says "Feed a puppy up to its appetite." Tootsie will eat when she is hungry. Your responsibility is to train her to be hungry when you fill her food bowl. If your dog has not finished its meal in thirty minutes, pick up its bowl. At the next normal feeding, fill the bowl as usual and set it out again. When attempting to set up a feeding schedule, don't allow the dog to have snacks between feedings.

Feeding by Age and Activity Level

Your pet's nutritional needs change as it matures. Amounts and times of feeding also depend on activity, climate, and physical condition. Young puppies, for instance, must be fed four to five times a day. The following information should help you to determine a proper feeding schedule for your dog.

Puppies Under Six Months of Age

A workable feeding schedule for a two- to three-month-old puppy is 7:00 A.M., Noon, 5:00 P.M., and 10:00 P.M. At this age offer the puppy a commercially mixed dry dog food, developed specifically for puppies, mixed with slightly warm water if you like.

Healthy puppies eat, sleep, eat, play, eat, tussle, and eat some more.

At age three months of age most puppies can sleep happily all night without the help of the 10:00 P.M. feeding. For the first few mornings after eliminating the night feeding, however, be prepared to offer breakfast a little earlier.

By the time the puppy is four months old its permanent teeth will begin to erupt. For the next three months, these itchy gums prompt the puppy to chew on almost anything. Dry crunchy dog food is preferred by this age group. Chew toys and bones offer some relief for aching gums.

Puppies Under One Year of Age

Puppies at the age of six months are entering into an active period of fully charged adolescence. Their protein and carbohydrate needs are high. Six- to 12-month-old puppies spend less time sleeping and expend more energy investigating their world. Meals can be cut down to twice a day. Six or seven months of age is also a good time to try self-feeding, which allows the puppy to adjust its intake as needed. Be careful that it doesn't get too fat. If it can't discipline itself as it self-feeds, go back to twice-a-day feeding.

Adult Dog

By the time Tootsie is 15 to 18 months old she will have reached a level of maturity that allows you to once more make changes in her diet. If you have not adopted self-feeding, continue a twice-a-day feeding schedule but change to a commercial diet that contains maintenance-level

Top left: Even if you don't intend to compete, basic training looks like fun.
Top right: Dedication and hard work pay off at the Broad Jump.
Bottom left: Up and over, and the High Jump is conquered with a lot of enthusiasm and no little amount of training.
Bottom right: A successful directed retrieve coming home. Is this the one you wanted?

proteins balanced for adult dogs. Tootsie herself may cut down to eating once a day. You will know when this happens, of course, because one meal will be left virtually uneaten. Try to follow her lead on this.

At this time many owners, recognizing that puppyhood is over, are tempted to bring their pet into the family, so to speak, and add table foods to its diet. You would be wise not to follow this practice. Your dog does not need "variety" in its diet. It does not get "tired of the same old thing." A dog can taste and smell every granule in its dish. Tootsie just doesn't like carrots. Try to slip a cooked carrot stick in a bowl of otherwise tasty stew and see if you don't find it rolling around in her bowl later, alone and neglected.

Pregnant and Nursing Bitches

The stress of pregnancy can take a toll on your dog's energy and health. It is extremely important to feed a pregnant bitch a diet higher in protein than usual. Many breeders return to puppy formulas because of this added need. Toward the end of her pregnancy, perhaps as soon as the seventh week, your dog may be too uncomfortable to eat large meals. You can help by offering smaller meals several times a day, or by providing a self-feeder.

After the litter arrives, the puppies receive nourishment from their mother for three to four weeks. This added burden on her system puts the mother under great nutritional stress. She will require more than twice the normal amounts of food. Here, too, a self-feeding system works well.

Top left: Good job, well done.
Top right: One reason they're called "springers."
Bottom left: A water retrieve is the most fun.
Bottom right: Pride and concentration win the day.

Older Dogs

Less energy leads to longer naps and a more sedentary life-style. Lessened activity allows extra calories to add pounds to a once handsome body. For older dogs, beginning at about the seventh year, the time has come to once again reduce the protein levels in its diet. With aging, all dogs develop some kidney dysfunction. This renal problem can be modified by offering a diet consisting of no more than 20 percent protein.

Worn or missing teeth can also cause problems. If your pet has trouble eating dry food, make an appointment with your veterinarian for a dental checkup. Meanwhile, try softening that food in warm water as you did when your dog was a puppy.

Overweight Dogs

Lowering Tootsie's fat intake while monitoring her caloric intake can add quality time to her

The canine senior citizen will appreciate a daily walk followed by a no-surprises, low-cal meal.

life. Veterinarians tell us that over 50 percent of the general dog population is overweight. Once again, as responsible owners, we can put our dogs on a diet easier than we can diet ourselves. Tootsie cannot open the pantry door and help herself to the cookies. Count every calorie, if necessary with the help of one of the low-calorie commercial foods. Increase her exercise level. Tootsie will appreciate it, will look better and live longer.

What Not to Feed Your Pet

"My dog is so fat he waddles. He can't help it that he loves fudge ripple ice cream. It's gotten so bad he won't let me eat until I give him a bowl, too," sighs one friend.

"When we go to the drive-in for lunch," adds another dog lover, "I order two burgers and two fries, one bag for me and one for my dog, Charlie."

"Once or twice a week, Buster and I sit down in front of the TV and chow down on a bag of chocolate bells," says another. "He loves them as much as I do."

What's wrong here? Are these pets loved or spoiled? As a pet owner you have a responsibility to see that your pet eats the right foods and stays away from the wrong ones. Particularly if your springer is overweight, or has special dietary needs, you must take charge of its diet.

Regardless of its weight, don't feed your springer:
• fried foods
• chocolate
• kernels of whole corn
• raw egg whites
• cakes
• pies
• desserts
• fish, chicken or pork bones

Ignore Tootsie's longing looks, sad eyes, and appealing gaze directed at a food that is not good for her. Instead, distract her with an offer of a more nourishing snack. Even though you are eating fried chips, Tootsie will be just as happy with a dog biscuit or a bit of cheese if she also receives your attention, a pat on the head, and a word of praise.

Puppy Kindergarten

Living with a dog trained to respond on command can be one of life's great pleasures. Living with a dog that ignores instructions or one that obeys occasionally can be a nightmare that can only get worse with time. The untrained dog is a nuisance to you and its neighborhood and a hazard to itself.

Begin puppy discipline in puppyhood. The training suggestions in this chapter are particularly useful for puppies three to seven months old. Wait to begin serious obedience training until your puppy is able to understand and respond to simple training routines. For most puppies, that understanding comes around the sixth or seventh month of life. Before that time, the puppy's enthusiasm will get in the way of its learning and you will both be discouraged. From three to six or seven months, teach puppy games, puppy kindergarten training, and puppy love.

A puppy, if not trained by its master, soon decides to train itself. That self-training is usually not what you had in mind. It is much more difficult to teach "yes" and "no" to an animal that has already decided to ignore "no." Even when properly trained, dogs reach a period of adolescent rebelliousness at about seven to nine months of age. Routines done to perfection one week are wildly imaginative the next. Just push through. Understanding will come.

Here are four basic guidelines: First, be observant. Not all springers respond in the same way to training. Take a long look at any previous training attempts, your dog's attitude, its preferences, its daily routines, and its willingness to please. Naturally willing, some springers have too much instinctive eagerness pushing them to be on the trail, so to speak, before they are ready for the journey.

Second, be patient. Likely, the procedures are new for both of you. Just remember, when working with your pet, give both corrections and rewards immediately to insure that the puppy links its infraction or its good behavior with your resulting reaction.

Third, have fun. Don't be harsh or vindictive even when aggravated beyond endurance. Make your corrections firmly but gently. If necessary, abandon the session. Start over again the next day, opening with a command your pet has mastered. Proceed from that command with a smile and the authority of one who cares.

Last, trainers agree that the adage "Practice makes perfect" is only partly correct. The motto should be, "Perfect practice makes perfect." Perfect practice is setting up regular training times, before meals is best, and sticking to them. Perfect practice time is fun. If you enjoy yourself your dog will have a good time, too. What is more, it will learn more quickly and look forward to working out with you. Perfect practice is teaching simple lessons and practicing them over and over again. Don't expect miracles. Keep in mind that if your dog understands what you expect and if at the same time it wants to please you, it will react as you wish.

Basic Training

Teaching a dog to understand what you want of it may be one of the hardest jobs you have ever attempted. Some pets and their masters never learn to communicate. When you both finally break through the barrier you can be justly proud of your accomplishments.

How and Why Springers Learn

Animal behaviorists tell us that our dogs learn by associating an action with a result. That is why immediate reaction on your part is so important. Correct or praise immediately after the fact. If you feel you are being forced to give an inappropriate amount of correction, try to prevent a misdeed in the first place. Try not to give a command that will not be obeyed. Don't give a "Come!" for instance, unless your puppy is on leash and you

Puppy Kindergarten

Obedience is a direct result of good communication which is a direct result of close companionship.

can coerce it to come if it doesn't come willingly. Don't give an "Off!" unless you are prepared to follow through and make it get off the sofa. Likewise, don't give a "Fetch!" or a "Down!"

Take advantage of the fact that springers naturally like to be with and to please their masters. They are at our side when we walk, at our feet when we sit down. They seem to ask little from us but our attention and sometimes not even that. Our presence is sufficient. When we try to leave them behind we are treated to the saddest and most reproachful eyes in creation.

Springers enjoy being useful. Bred to work, to hunt, to accompany their masters in the field, and curious by nature, springers can become so agitated at the prospect of a walk in unexplored country that unless leashed they will bound from the car propelled by new aromas and new fields to

conquer. A springer can be so stimulated the night before a trip by the sight of hunting gear taken from the closet and put in the car that it is physically unable to sleep.

We are told that dogs have no sense of the future, do not understand our motivations, do not understand our language and never will. They, nevertheless,

• do remember people and experiences in total detail.

• do recognize tones of voice and facial expressions.

• do understand kindness and respond to it with obedience and lifelong devotion.

Use this hard-earned knowledge when you work with your dog.

Who's the Boss?

Some behavior is instinctive, bred into your dog through the years to produce certain traits. Some German shepherds are bred to be guard dogs. Some spaniels are bred to be companionable lapdogs. Your springer possesses a basic instinct for hunting that helps it to be a better bird dog than a dalmatian, a better swimmer than a Chihuahua, and a faster runner than a dachshund. Yet, all of these dogs—the German shepherd, the spaniel, the dalmatian, the Chihuahua, and the dachshund—share one basic instinct. None of these dogs will willingly live alone. Each has a need to be part of a pack. When you take a puppy away from its natural relatives and introduce it to your own family, that family becomes its pack.

When training and working with your springer, you should remember two important aspects of pack behavior. First, each pack has one leader. Second, there is no such position as coleader. You either are the boss or you are not. When you and your springer train, one of you will be the leader. It is up to you to assume the role.

As leader, your first job is to be certain your dog obeys every command you give. Insist on obedience. Don't give a command unless you can reinforce it. If you find you have to physically put the dog in a "Down," for instance, don't hesitate to do so. For most of us, this means working on a leash until you are sure the dog will obey.

Your Training Tools

Basically, you will use four tools: two collars and two leashes. A flat collar and basic six-foot (2 m) leash are used for everyday handling. A metal slip-chain collar is added during training sessions. A 20- to 30-foot long (6–10 m) leash or line is indispensable for controlling your pet when out of doors teaching "Come," for instance.

Dog Collars

By the time Sandy has completed his basic puppy shots (at about four months of age) you will surely want him to be accustomed to a collar. Your veterinarian probably has a supply and can make a recommendation. Flat, buckled collars are easily sized. Try one on your dog. If you can slip three fingers between your pet's neck and the collar it is sized just right. Check the fit often because the growing puppy will outgrow the collar before you know it. Flat nylon webbed or lightweight leather collars are inexpensive and appropriate for puppies.

A lightweight slip-chain metal training collar, commonly called a choke chain collar, will be one of your most valuable training tools. The common name choke is misleading. Properly used, the collar will not choke your pet but will get its attention. The collar could properly be called a check collar because the purpose is to check (stop) an activity. Be sure to remove the collar after each session and replace it with a flat, buckled collar. Free running pets have been strangled when choke chain collars catch on fences, branches, or other obstacles in the field.

Using a Choke Chain Collar: Attach the leash to the collar. Hold the free ring of the collar in your left hand. Using your right hand, pick up the hanging chain of the collar and drop a section of the chain (with the leash still attached) through the free ring. Widen the resulting circle. Face your dog. Hold the collar and leash so that the shape resembles a capital letter "P" with the leash on the left, forming the stem of the "P." Pull the choke collar over your dog's head letting the leash fall free down the right side of the dog's neck.

Adjust the collar so that it sits high on your dog's neck, just behind the ears. Check the position by giving a strong pull on the leash. If the collar is properly set it will tighten immediately and loosen as immediately when you release the pressure. This is very important. The choke collar must hang free when the dog is performing as expected. An improperly applied collar, one that is always tight, is of no use in training.

Leash

Metal leashes are often too heavy for a young springer. Either a leather or a webbed leash about

Playtime, quiet time, school time. Spend quality time with your friend.

Puppy Kindergarten

6 feet (2 m) long is satisfactory. Because some leather leashes are also too heavy and because the webbed leashes are light and colorful, the latter are often first choice.

To hold the leash correctly, put your right thumb through the loop. Fold and keep a tight hold of all but an arm's length of leash in your right hand. (The leash comes out of your grasp near your little finger.) Place your left hand on the leash immediately next to your right hand. If the collar rings are together and the leash snap is hanging down, the leash is on correctly. Hold your elbows close to your body slightly below waist level.

Whistle

Many trainers cultivate a whistle to call in their dogs. Those unable to summon a loud enough whistle often purchase slim silver-toned whistles and hang them around their necks at training times. Used mostly in conjunction with the "Come" command, the whistle can be a very helpful training adjunct.

Food as Reward

You are trying to train your dog that a command from you requires a certain action on its part. When your pet acts appropriately, be quick with a positive response. Although several well-respected trainers insist that a dog must work for a kind word alone, there is nothing basically wrong with offering your dog a treat for a job well done. Bites of liver, dog biscuits, and cheese are rewards that, when offered at the proper time, help you to say "Good job." When reinforced by verbal praise, playtime, hugs, and pats, food treats become a part of positive motivation. Your dog will learn that love, discipline, and treats all come from the same source.

A problem arises when the concept of a special reward is carried too far and the treat is both anticipated and expected. Because there will be many times when you want your dog to obey without any incentive except a desire to please you, be sure your pup receives plenty of hugs and verbal praise, too.

On the subject of treats, showdogs are selected partly for their conformation (how good they look) and partly for their enthusiasm. That enthusiasm is often enhanced by treats offered by a handler. Watch the eyes of a showdog sparkle as it anticipates a bit of liver. Watch closely at the next conformation show. Savvy handlers keep these boiled treats at instant readiness hidden in their jacket pockets, folded into a long sleeve, or tucked like snuff into their own cheeks.

One recipe that has proven a favorite on the show and training circuit follows:
8 oz. (1 kg) beef liver
2 tsp. (10 g) garlic powder
1 tsp. (5 g) salt
2 cups (235 ml) water
Dice liver into ½-inch (1 cm) cubes. Add salt and garlic powder and liver to the water. Bring water mixture to a rolling boil. Reduce heat and simmer 25 minutes or until the liver is fork tender. Remove from heat, drain, and cool. Refrigerate. Will keep up to two weeks.

Voice and Body Signals

Many of us believe a properly motivated springer puppy can understand many more words than was once thought. It is known an adult springer can respond to at least twenty command words. It is important that these words be short, positive, and distinguishable. Avoid using the same word for two situations. This happens most frequently with the command word "Down." If you use "Down" to mean "Lie down on the floor," don't use "Down" when you want your puppy off the sofa or to stop jumping on people, for instance. The commands "Off!" and "No jumping!" work well for those situations.

The five most frequently used commands are referred to as the mantra of basic obedience. These five commands are "Sit," "Come," "Stay," "Heel," and "Down." For best results, don't use these command words for any situation other than to initiate basic obedience routines.

In addition to the mantra of five, other commands your springer can learn to respond to are "Watch," "Enough," "Okay," "No more," "Off," "Give," "Drop it," "Good," "Move," "Out," "Take it," "Leave it," "Jump in," "No jumping," "Kennel-up," "Let's go," "Hurry up," and "Wait."

To release your dog from any command, give it a couple of quick pats on the chest and a warm "Okay!"

Tone of Voice

Your dog connects the words you say with your body language and the tone of your voice in order to understand your meaning. Voice change is natural. Most animal lovers change their tone of voice when speaking to a favorite pet. They have learned that intimate, crooning tones, for instance, cause their pet's ears to perk up. Often that pet will sit, head cocked to one side, as it listens.

Successful dog handlers cultivate two distinct changes of tone when speaking to a dog. Praise is best offered in a happy, loving, sing-song tone of voice quite unlike a normal speaking voice. Corrections are given in a stern no-nonsense tone of final authority. Whether you are teaching the official obedience commands or one of those designed to make everyday living more comfortable, cultivate your own training voices. Practice those voices until they become natural to you.

Body Language

When you praise your springer, be happy and be sure you convey that happiness to your pet.

Some trainers jump up and down, others clap their hands and applaud enthusiastically. Others offer a treat for a job well done and give their pet a pat on the head and a rub under the chin.

On the other hand, when their pets must be disciplined, these savvy trainers have learned to turn away, avert their eyes, correct their dogs in a low, disappointed tone of voice or even a growl.

Teaching Basic Obedience in Six Weeks

Some dog owners say that if their dog just learns to come when called, they will be satisfied. Actually, though, because the obedience commands are built on a structure each reinforces the other. "Come" is one of the most difficult commands to teach. "Sit," on the other hand, can be taught to puppies three months old and even younger.

When teaching these commands, follow six guidelines:

1. Work on the commands in the order listed below: "Sit," "Heel," "Stay," "Come," and "Down." Work on one new command a week. Each week add the next command and review the previous commands.
2. Hold training sessions five days a week, twice a day for 15 to 20 minutes each time. Have fun.
3. To be sure your dog will obey you, begin each of these commands with your pet on a leash. Don't attempt any of these off-leash until you are confident you will be obeyed.
4. Correct your dog before it has a chance to disobey or ignore you. Some trainers jump in and correct if they even suspect a problem of inattention.
5. Precede the moving commands ("Down" and "Heel,") with your dog's name. When you give a stationary command ("Sit," "Stay," and "Down") omit your dog's name. Thus you would say, "Sandy, heel!" or "Sandy, come!" but "Stay."

6. This last suggestion is difficult to follow, but very important. DON'T REPEAT A COMMAND. Your dog heard you the first time. Once is enough. If your dog hasn't responded, go to the dog and physically make it obey (push on it, pull it, lift it, whatever) without giving the command a second time. The idea behind this rule is that you don't want Sandy to decide to wait for time number three, or to wait until a certain amount of growling and exasperation enters your voice. If growling is what it takes to make your dog obey, re-think your training voice. Sound exasperated the first time.

The "Sit" Command

"Sit," a useful, easy-to-learn command, is known as the attention-getting command. Your dog learns to sit while anticipating the next command.

Hold the leash in your right hand close to the collar and put your springer on your left side. You will be standing next to your dog with both of you facing straight ahead. Say "sit." (Do not use your dog's name.) Simultaneously pull up on the leash with your right hand and stroke the dog's back

Praise your puppy for a good "Sit."

with your left hand, eventually pushing down on the dog's hindquarters if necessary. When your dog sits, pet it and praise it. Invite it to play for a minute or two before going on to another lesson or before trying that one again. "What a good dog! You are the best puppy! I never had such a wonderful puppy!"

The puppy should hold a sit position for several seconds before being released with an "Okay." If it starts to move before the "Okay," say "no!" and pull up on the leash. Wait several more seconds, give an "Okay" and praise your pet. Give it a treat at this time if you like.

Within a day or two you won't have to push on the dog's hindquarters any longer. Instead, you can use your left hand to teach the hand signal for "Sit": Extend your left arm straight in front of you, above your dog's eye level. Point your index finger toward your pet while saying "sit."

The "Heel" Command

An aimless stroll on a starry night, or a walk off-leash through the woods or field on a wonderfully sunny day can be heaven for you and your dog. But because most of our dog walking is on a busy street or in a town or neighborhood with strict leash laws, we can't walk off-leash as often as we would like. One of the benefits of teaching our pets to enjoy walking at heel is that even when walking on-leash we can offer them as much of that sense of companionship and freedom as possible.

First, sit your dog at your left side (the heel position), its head even with your left knee. Attach the leash and the choke chain. Hold the leash in your right hand. Call your dog's name. Say "Sandy, heel." At that same moment, start off on your left foot. Give a light jerk on the leash. Pat your leg. Move briskly. Keep the lead as short and slack as possible.

Be enthusiastic. Assume Sandy will want to come walking with you. Keep up a stream of animated patter, "Good boy, aren't we having fun? Sandy's a good dog! Look at us go! Let's go walking, you and me, just a bit more, good boy, here we go." Walk in a straight line. Your puppy will be excited and will forge ahead to investigate new smells or will head out on his own exploration and veer into you. Just nudge him over, keep on walking, talk to him to keep him interested. For the first lessons, you're both doing fine if you can walk at least ten paces without generating any leash tension.

If you have to correct your puppy, and you will, correct quickly with a short, downward snap on the leash. "Check, release, and praise," my first teacher said. "Be quick about it, snap and release." In other words, make the correction and keep on walking. Sandy will look up at you as if to ask if you felt that sudden pull, too. Act as if you had nothing to do with that momentary tightening of the collar around its neck. Your puppy will figure out that when it doesn't pay attention, something strange happens. When Sandy does watch you, you make him feel good. Walk on, talking to him, "Good boy, that's the way, come on, Sandy, let's go as far as that tree, come on, now, let's go, here we go, good boy."

In later lessons, practice turning, circling, cornering, and walking among other dogs and people. Always practice on-leash. Don't move to off-leash until you are confident your puppy will follow your every step—and that may take months. You may be sure that if Sandy won't walk under control on a loose leash he is not ready for off-leash heeling. Even then carry the leash with you to slip back on at the first sign of insurrection.

The "Stay" Command

Once again, sit your puppy on your left, in heel position, both of you facing straight ahead. Hold a tight leash in your left hand. Now bring your right hand in front of your dog's face (like a traffic patrolman's "Stop" signal) and push that hand, palm forward, toward the puppy, saying "Stay!" Using your right foot, step out and stop directly in front of your dog. Which foot you use to step out with is an important point, because your pet should be watching your left foot expecting a signal to heel. Keep your eye on your dog, count to ten, and then step back to the heel position. Release the pressure on the leash, say "okay," and praise your puppy. Praise it whether it really did okay or not. You may have had to return to your dog once or twice to reinforce the command, but in the end, before the lesson was concluded, it did stay, so praise joyously. Release your dog. Play games. Throw a stick down the path. Race to see who gets to the stick first. (You lose.) Have fun. Smile and laugh and be enthusiastic. Speak warmly to your dog: "Good boy, Sandy, good job! What a good time we are having!" (If you get even a 30-second stay at this point in your training you both deserve a fun time.)

"Stay" right here and wait for me.

For the next lesson, still on-leash, gradually increase the distance between you and your puppy. Move back, perhaps 3 feet this time, and again give the command "Stay!" If that works as you expect it to, move 6 feet farther away the following week and try again. Remember, when your puppy does as you command be ready with hugs and pats and praise. Eventually, maybe next week—maybe the week after that—if all is progressing nicely, try "Stay" without the leash. Be ready, though, to step in with a correction the moment your dog even glances away.

Remember that the purpose of "Stay" is to get your dog to wait for you, so if he moves or if you even think he is about to move, step right in with a firm correction. Say "No! Stay!" in a stern tone.

By the end of six weeks your dog should stay off-leash at least six minutes. Eventually, you can work up to moving out of sight, or going into the house for a few minutes and expecting your puppy to stay. The dog won't be thrilled, but it is able to stay and it should.

The "Come" Command

The fun command, "Come" is called the command that must be obeyed. "Come" also must be learned on-leash. If your puppy learns that it can disobey "Come" you will have a difficult time enforcing it later. Precede the command with your dog's name, as you did with "Heel."

The whistle signal for "Come" is a series of beep-beep-beeps. Start whistling immediately after you give the command and continue the whole time the dog is coming toward you.

Because "Come" is a command that must be obeyed, make that command attractive. Try kneeling down and clapping your hands. Hold your arms out as a welcome. Hug your dog when it arrives, give it lots of praise and a really tasty treat. When you are training for "Come," always have a pat, a kind word, a treat, or all three for that happy puppy. Make that puppy believe that coming to you is much more fun than not coming.

Two very important points about "Come" training:

- Never correct or discipline your dog after it has finally come. The dog will not understand the correction. In its mind, it came to you and you fussed at it.
- Never ignore your springer when it comes to you following a "Come" command. Pat it, hug it, talk to it, give it a good rub under the chin or between the ears, and make it happy that it came.

The "Down" Command

Some springers have a difficult time with "Down" because it is against their nature to be subservient. Because you are expecting to see some form of subservience, don't let the "Down" command become a battle of wills unless you plan to win.

Again, this command is learned on-leash. Put Sandy in the sit position. Hold the leash in your left hand leaving several feet of the leash still on the floor. Move out with your right foot until you are standing in front of the puppy. Once again bring your right hand in front of your dog's face (remember the traffic patrolman's "Stop" signal) but this time as you give the "Down" command, move your hand down toward the floor. Say "dow-n-n-n."

There are several good methods for teaching "Down." Select one and be ready to try another if that doesn't work. Primarily, you are trying to force your dog to associate an action with a command. You might carefully pull Sandy's front paws forward, while pushing on his shoulders thereby forcing him into a prone position. You might place the leash under your foot and pull the puppy down while giving the command. Experiment with the command. Be careful with this command. Don't get very loud and annoyed, don't get very forceful with the pressure. You don't want to frighten your dog. Be gentle, be aware, and offer plenty of praise and affection. Soon enough your dog will learn "Down" and you will both have progressed nicely in your training.

The Canine Good Citizen Award

In an effort to stem the American public's increasing unhappiness with stray, untrained, and unreliable neighborhood dogs, some responsible trainers devised a course designed to produce a Canine Good Citizen (CGC).

The course, offered over a period of six to eight weeks, is usually sponsored by local all-breed clubs, humane societies, and 4-H Clubs. The lessons, often held in neighborhood parks, on school playgrounds, and in shopping centers, conclude with a ten-point test designed to measure the dog's basic manners. Those dogs passing the test receive a certificate certifying that they demonstrated appropriate behavior in public with people and with other dogs. The program has received great public acceptance and its graduates are recognized by many organizations. Therapy Dogs International, for instance, will not accept a dog for further training until it is CGC-certified.

In CGC training, dogs are required to earn a passing grade for each of the following requirements:

1. *Appearance and grooming:* In addition to the obvious well-cared for appearance, dogs must possess up-to-date vaccinations.
2. *Accepting a stranger:* The dog must allow a stranger to approach its handler without growling or snapping or evidencing aggressive behavior.
3. *Walk on a loose lead:* Walking at heel at its handler's left side, the dog must demonstrate the ability to stop, turn, and follow.
4. *Walk through a crowd:* The dog should be able to move among pedestrian traffic without difficulty.
5. *Sit for exam:* Again, the dog must allow a stranger to approach, this time also permit petting, without reacting aggressively.
6. *Sit and Down on command:* In response to the handler's commands, the dog should adequately demonstrate familiarity with the concepts of "Sit" and "Down."
7. *Stay in position:* The dog must demonstrate that it can remain in position (sitting or lying down) when commanded to do so.
8. *Reaction to another dog:* The dog is allowed to become aware of other dogs but it must not display any aggressiveness toward them.
9. *Reaction to distractions:* Although aware of and interested in the situation, the dog must not disobey a command.
10. *Dog left alone:* The dog is expected to be able to handle a five-minute tie-out without becoming unduly upset.

Teaching Livable, Practical Habits

There is no secret to teaching a dog to obey, and there is only one rule: Be sure you and your dog are speaking the same language. Each of the following commands is a common sense procedure. Be sure your puppy is ready to learn and play before you start.

The "Leave It" Command

When you want your puppy to drop an object it is carrying or to cease investigating an intriguing odor use "Leave it." This command is also appropriate when you want your puppy to wait for permission to accept a treat instead of lunging for it. Put your dog in a sit using the left hand index finger as a reminder. Say sternly, "Leave it!" Remove the object with your hand and drop it to the ground. Do not let the dog pick it up again until you release it with a quick "Okay!"

Puppy Kindergarten

The "Give" Command

When you want your dog to place an object in your hand, a stick or glove it has retrieved, for instance, hold your hand out and say "Give!" Take the object from the dog if necessary by tapping it lightly under the chin. Don't get into a tug of war.

Be careful with "Give." Don't use the command every single time the puppy retrieves. Puppies tire easily, and they particularly hate to hand over their hard-won treasures. Allow your puppy to run off and snuggle down with its treasure occasionally.

The "Off" Command

When you want your pet off the sofa or off your easy chair, or to stop jumping on you, remember not to use the command "Down." Save this important command for "lie down on the floor," or "lie down and wait for me." Substitute "Off!" instead of "Down" for "get off the chair." If necessary—and it will be necessary in the beginning—give the command, and when your puppy stares at you like you must be mistaken, help it off the sofa. The moment all four feet are on the floor, praise your dog for following orders. Help the puppy find a place to lie down that is equally (well, almost) comfortable and more acceptable. A floor pillow, a rug behind the chair, or its own crate are good alternates.

Hurry Up

Some dog owners have tried to find another phrase for their dog's act of elimination instead of "let's go potty," "do your business," or "time to tinkle." Your dog doesn't particularly care which words you use—or which language you use, for that matter. (I had some Shar-pei friends who knew how to say "go potty" in Chinese.) If you want to use a customary family saying, or to make one up, by all means go ahead.

Some of us feel comfortable using "hurry up." When your dog asks to be let out or when you take your puppy outside, say "let's hurry up and go outside," (or to the paper, or wherever). When the puppy begins to eliminate, say "hurry up!" (As far as we know this hasn't backfired as when "hurry up" is also used following "get off the sofa.") Don't forget to praise the puppy whatever words you use.

Go to Bed

Many of my family's visitors, professed dog lovers all, object to sharing the couch with a pet, strenuously object to having it curl up at their feet, and certainly don't want it leaning against their legs. My mother, not a dog lover but at least amiably tolerant of our pets, taught every one of them, "that's enough." After they greeted her, sniffed around for a treat, and were just settling down to visit, she would draw her hand away and say, "that's ENOUGH!" They soon learned to go find some other feet to curl up around or they would be sent "to bed."

In my home, the dog's beds are multiple. Our dogs could have a bed in several rooms. A rug next to a recliner, a crate in the laundry room or a pillow in the living room corner. We point to the particular bed we would like to see them in at the time. When they are puppies, we carry them to their crate after saying "go to bed." When we have company, while we eat, or whenever our pets are underfoot a quick "go to your bed" allows them to remain in the room and be part of the family. Very few visitors object to the presence of a family dog resting quietly in a corner of the room.

Shake Hands

Tell your puppy, "Shake," then pick up its right paw and shake it. (Because studies show that the majority of dogs are what we would call right-handed and because most people expect a right-hand shake, teach the puppy to offer the right paw by not accepting a left paw offer. Say "No!" Don't touch the puppy's left paw, say "Shake!" again and lift the right paw if necessary.) If you have to pick up the paw, shake it and praise the puppy just as highly as if it had handed you the paw without help. Say "Good puppy, Sandy, what a good puppy," or whatever affectionate line you feel comfortable with. Give the puppy half of a dog biscuit, a bite of cheese, or a bit of liver. Repeat this activity at various times through the week. Your bright-eyed puppy will learn quickly to raise its paw.

Correcting Bad Habits

Bad habits, once established, are hard to break. Without realizing it, you could even contribute to the problem if you fail to make clear to the dog what you are asking it to rectify. Certainly this is true if you correct long after the fact. The young puppy just can't figure out which of its activities upset you. Your best approach in puppyhood is prevention.

Usually, if the mischief occurred out of your sight or earlier in the day, you can do little to correct it. You can fuss, but it won't prevent a recurrence. Be on guard for a similar infraction when you are at home. When you see your pet get into mischief use the opportunity to teach a lesson. Jump in right away with scoldings and discipline.

Although no one method will work with all problems, the following suggestions are part of the same theory. The method employed depends on you, your dog, and the immediacy of the discipline.
- Get your dog's attention; surprise is good.
- Correct and discipline immediately.
- Let the dog know you're disappointed.
- Distract the dog with a toy, a game, or playtime.
- Praise the dog for minding you.

Chewing

Sometime around the third month of life a puppy's permanent teeth will begin to emerge. Most puppies are considerably bothered by this process, gnawing and gumming their way through your treasures. Because the teething process can last from 7 to 18 months, this discomfort bothers us as well.

Left to its own devices a teething puppy will chew on any comforting object—a table leg, the front steps, or the rungs of your grandmother's rocker. The first time you catch your puppy chewing the back porch steps say "No!" Next, move the puppy to a new location and quickly offer its favorite chew toy. Return to the porch steps and sprinkle the site with hot pepper sauce or cayenne pepper or a commercially prepared bitter apple liquid just in case you are not around the next time the puppy gets the urge to gnaw wood.

Be observant. When your puppy tires of the chew toy it may bypass those now nasty-smelling porch steps and head for a tasty chair leg instead. Say "No!", rap the puppy lightly under the chin this time, then move it to a new location and again offer a chew toy substitute.

Puppies aren't the sole culprits here. Older dogs will also chew because of boredom, anxiety, nutritional deficiency, or lack of exercise. The remedy is the same. Say "No!", distract the dog, pepper the object, check its diet, and offer a chewable substitute.

Wooden objects are not the only objects a young dog may like to chew. A puppy, not realizing the sharpness of that new set of teeth, will nibble at your fingers or tug at your ankles when it gets excited. Don't allow this type of behavior. Those are your fingers, and the puppy will eventually bite down hard enough to draw blood on you or a guest.

Say "No!" and move your hand away. If the puppy continues nibbling, say "No!" Hold its mouth shut and—using one finger—lightly rap it under the chin or on the nose. Stop playing with the puppy. Pick it up and move it to another area. Give it something else to play with and leave it alone. In a few minutes, come back and praise the puppy for being good. Act as though you forgot all about the problem. The puppy has.

Biting

Your puppy may growl at you when you correct it. It may even snarl when you remove your shoes from its mouth. Accept none of this behavior. Don't forgive these incidents with "it's just a puppy" balm. Correct and recondition your pet immediately.

Many family adult dogs will bite if provoked. A dog that has been trained to guard and protect property or people will bite if instructed to do so. A territorial family dog will bite strange people and other dogs because of possessiveness. A frightened dog will bite if it is in pain.

Some adult dogs with unchecked aggression will bite without provocation. These animals are a danger to society and a disgrace to their owners. Allowing such dogs to run loose is irresponsible because they can pose a serious threat to public safety; moreover their owners could be held ethically, morally, and financially liable for the consequences of their pet's behavior.

Jumping Up

If you do not wish your puppy to jump on your guests or on you unless commanded to do so, begin training early. Train on soft ground, not on a concrete driveway or sidewalk because your intention is to cause the puppy to lose its balance. When your dog comes at you and appears ready to jump up, say "No jumping!" and briskly raise your knee toward its chest. Act unconcerned when the dog tumbles backwards as though you have no idea how it got in such an awkward position. Call the puppy to you, stoop down, and love it. Tell it what a good puppy it is. Walk away.

Repeat the lesson each time your dog attempts a jump. Be careful not to let the dog think the accident was anybody's fault but its own. A very few unexpected somersaults will teach a bright springer not to jump.

Some trainers suggest stepping on an adult dog's hind feet while saying "No jumping!" This will not be necessary if you train the dog as a puppy. Anyway, for most of us a springer's hind feet are out of comfortable reach.

Some owners of smaller breeds train their pets to jump into their arms on command. Unhappy with the prospect of a spring-loaded 50-pound dog landing unexpectedly, and aware that even the best trained dogs can't tell the difference between good clothes and training clothes, some springer owners teach their dogs a similar, less jubilant command: The dog learns to rise on command on its back legs, placing its paws on the owner's waist. The dog is then given a hearty ear and chin rub or a treat. With few exceptions, this command cures unexpected jumping because it keeps you in control. You, in effect, invite the dog up when you want it up.

Barking

Very few habits are as annoying as unrestrained barking. Dogs will bark at unusual noises, bark from loneliness, bark at a rising moon, and sometimes bark just from the sheer joy of joining a neighborhood chorus. If you are at home, open the door and call "No barking!" Call your pet to you and give it a pat and a hug for coming. Remember, don't discipline the dog when it comes to you because the canine mind will make the wrong association. "I was out having a lot of fun," it thinks, "but you called me so I quit what I was doing to come to you. Boy, were you in a bad mood! I'm not going to come so quickly next time!"

If your dog continues to bark and is annoying you and the neighborhood, be prepared with some annoying tricks of your own. Think of ways to startle the dog so that instead of receiving satisfaction from barking, he receives an unpleasant surprise.

If the dog is inside the house, and there is a door between you, try startling the dog by rapping sharply on the door every time the noise starts. If your dog is out of doors barking at the neighborhood strays, open the door and call him to you. "Sandy, come!" Sometimes, your dog is barking on "automatic" and this distraction will work wonders. Pet him and put him back out again. You had to get up, but at least you went back to sleep.

If you are gone during the day and have close neighbors who (rightly) complain about your barking dog, the solution is more complicated. Try to determine the cause of the outbreak and eliminate it. If the barking is caused by the arrival of the postman or a delivery person enlist the aid of the complaining neighbor.

Pretend to leave as usual and ask your neighbor to come up to the door in the manner of the delivery person. When your dog barks, you appear and scold him. "No barking!" Several unpleasant surprises like an unhappy master can distract even the most dedicated barker.

Chasing Cars

Car chasing is dangerous. Hyperactive dogs, bored dogs and dogs with inbred hunting instincts, love to chase cars. All are a nuisance to the neighborhood and a hazard to themselves.

If your dog chases cars, and fencing your property or confining the dog isn't practical, enlist the help of a friend with a car, preferably a car unknown to your pet. Hide in the back seat with the window rolled down. Have your friend drive by at a normal speed. When your dog begins the chase, jump up, lean out the window and command "No! Go home!" The dog should be so perplexed he will slink away for the day.

For truly dedicated car chasers, one surprise is not enough. One well-known trainer suggests that you invest in a squirt bottle. Fill the bottle with plain water. Ask two friends (who each have access to a car) to give you a few minutes of their time one afternoon. (You don't have to be in the car this time, you can be in the house, looking out the window.) Ask one friend to drive and the other to hide in the back seat. When the dog begins its chase ask the driver to command "No!" Have the friend in the back seat give your dog a good squirt of water in the face.

About ten minutes later, ask your friends to exchange cars and positions (it's the car we want Sandy to dislike, not your friends) and to follow the same procedure. The lesson should be learned: Cars are attractive but there's something dangerous about them.

If squirt bottles and commands don't work you may have an inveterate car chaser on your hands and you'll have to tie up the dog or fence it in for its own safety.

Canine College

If our springers graduate from Puppy Kindergarten, most of us are well pleased. For those who wish to provide a "higher" education, however, the springer national breed club, local all-breed organizations, and how-to literature are as close as your telephone.

The Worlds of AKC and UKC

Two primary organizations provide information and registration for the springer spaniel.

The American Kennel Club is a nonprofit organization comprised of almost 400 dog clubs throughout the United States. The Club's primary purpose is to foster interest in the health and welfare of purebred dogs while maintaining a dog registry for its member clubs.

The AKC monthly publishes the *Pure-Bred Dogs American Kennel Gazette* magazine designed to help the clubs communicate, but it also highlights the latest veterinary, training, and legislative news.

The United Kennel Club maintains a registry comprised of 166 breeds of working dogs. The UKC registry divides breeds into eight groups: Guardian Dogs, Scenthounds, Sighthounds, Gun Dogs, Northern Breeds, Herding Dogs, Terriers, and Companion Dogs. The English springer spaniel is a member of the Gun Dog group. The UKC publishes three useful and widely respected magazines, each aimed at a particular need: *Bloodlines, Coonhound Bloodlines* and *Hunting Retriever.*

The World of ESSFTA

Within these worlds, and an integral part of them, are thousands of breed clubs each devoted to the promotion of one species. In 1924 and 1925, a group of pheasant hunters who admired the springer's abilities in the field, formed an association designed to encourage the breed. Interested in promoting the springer as the versatile hunting dog it is, these men drew up a breed standard and in 1926 submitted it to the AKC. As the first springer club to join the AKC, the English Springer Spaniel Field Trial Association (ESSFTA) is known as the "parent" club. The association, representing the collective springer breed clubs, has a voice in AKC policy and decision making.

The ESSFTA sponsors several prominent, well-attended events each year. The National Specialty Show, a conformation show, promotes and honors the show springer. In addition, it sponsors the Parent Club Field Trials held the last weekend in October and the National Amateur Championship.

Field Trials

A field trial is a course designed to simulate natural hunting conditions. Basically, the dogs are expected to flush a game bird and, on command, to retrieve it without damage. The tests are competitive, pitting dogs of a similar breed disposition against each other in as close to possible normal hunting conditions.

The National English Springer Spaniel Field Trial Association, founded in 1947, primarily is responsible for conducting a licensed field trial each year during the last week of November and the first week of December. At that time the winning springer is designated National Springer Spaniel Field Champion.

Top left: A handsome representation of the breed.
Top right: Obedient, attentive, and even-tempered, the springer is a master showman.
Bottom left: Eyes up, pay attention, now.
Bottom right: A working dog and a friend, the springer is an amiable companion at the end of a long day.

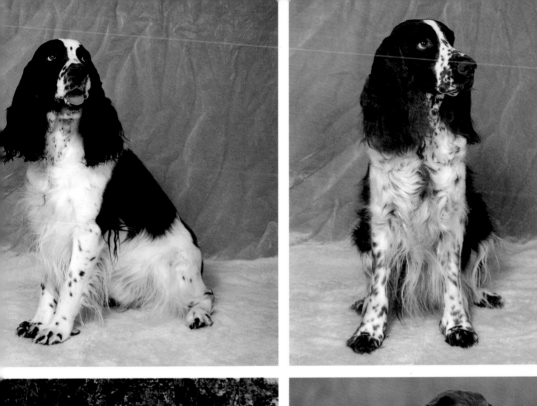

Showing Off

Some say there are two types of springers: family-type show springers and family-type hunting springers. The statement points out the fact that this breed's owners are devoted to its stay-at-home personality as well as to its exceptional hunting abilities. On the other hand, it is also true that for years the two basic types have been regarded as almost separate breeds, so far apart are the lines. Most springers look handsome, especially when brushed, and most springers love to hunt, but not for years has a top gundog springer also placed top on the show circuit. Some attribute this lack of duality to the field dog's high, excitable temperament, the very temperament that makes it a top field dog. Others say the owner showing in conformation will not risk that beautiful coat to the burrs and scrapes of the field.

Accepting it as a given that each type has its place in the hearts of owners, how does one go about demonstrating that this family-type dog has few equals?

Conformation: Training Your Springer to Show

Take a look at your puppy's official pedigree some day. If several of its ancestors had the designation, "Ch." preceding their names you can be sure they and their handlers worked hard to gain the honor of Champion of Record. Showing your dog in conformation can be fulfilling and self-satisfying. Conformation means how closely your dog matches the official standard of the breed.

Top: Now it's showtime, and with it the challenge of demonstrating poise and beauty.
Bottom: Another kind of showtime, for another audience, and another demonstration of hard-earned skills.

Show time can be fun for both of you.

That standard is discussed in the chapter Understanding Springer Spaniels. If your springer matches the standard and in addition matches it better than any other springer present that day, that fact will be recognized by the judge. You will reap the reward of having your judgment confirmed by others who are knowledgeable about the breed.

Dog Shows

Putting on a big dog show is big business. Nationwide, the business of dog shows is the province of a handful of specialists called superintendents. These professionals coordinate show schedules to avoid geographic conflicts, mail notices (called premium lists) and receive applications, supply necessary ring equipment, and submit the results to the sponsoring organization. Individuals wishing to participate in an upcoming licensed show can ask to be put on a mailing list. Information on superintendents, show scheduling, and sponsorship can be obtained from most local breed club members and often from your veterinarian.

You will find two types of licensed conformation shows listed in the premium lists. Entries may be confined to a single breed, the English springer spaniel, for instance. These are called specialty shows. The all-breed show is, as its name suggests, open to any AKC-registered breed.

In either show, dogs are judged on how closely they match the all-important breed standard. The standards clearly state what is and is not to be faulted. Movement, physical condition, and attitude are part of the standard. Even though judges presently may be or were at some time breeders and are known to have preferences for "a good head," for instance, or "fluffy ears" they must adhere to the rules and are not to indulge their individual tendencies. The decision is not supposed to be subjective; that is, the dog is to be judged on what it is like on a particular day, not what it will be, who its dam was, or how many points it has earned already. Nevertheless, the time of day, the number of entries, the weather, all enter into the final decision.

Making a Champion

The Westminster Kennel Club Dog Show, held annually in New York City's Madison Square Garden, is considered the nation's premier all-breed dog show. In the first chapter we met Robert, the English springer spaniel named Best in Show at Westminster 1993. Perhaps you would be interested learning the steps your springer wold be expected to climb in order to achieve that honor.

To become an American Kennel Club champion a dog must compete against other dogs of the same breed for points. Dogs can receive from one to five points at a particular show. The point structure is coordinated according to breed, sex, number of dogs in competition, and geographical location of the show. The structure is periodically adjusted by the AKC, usually as a result of that breed's regional ascent or descent in popularity.

To earn its championship (become a Champion of Record) a dog must receive a total of 15 points. On at least two occasions the points must have been awarded against significant competition (at three-, four-, or five-point shows.) In addition, the dog must receive those 15 points from at least three different judges. Point show judges are approved by the national association. Before approval the applicants are tested on their working knowledge of the breed and their clear regard for the standard.

A five-point major show for English springers in one region of the states, for instance, might require a field of 25 whereas only 15 entries might be necessary in a part of the country where fewer are in competition. A one-point show, on the other hand, could consist of only two male dogs. Consequently, handlers trying to finish their dogs often drive miles each weekend frequently spending an entire season on the "circuit" in search of the major show that will bring with it that magic title. The excitement of a five-point major win somehow makes the long driving days, the burdensome packing and repacking, the time spent away from family, somehow worth the trouble.

Step One—The Entry Classes

The incoming entries are divided by sex and then classified according to age, breeding, and handling qualifications. Basically, the five classifications for each sex are as follows:

- *Puppy Class:* Dogs older than six months and younger than one year.
- *Novice Class:* Dogs older than six months who have not won prizes and points in this or other classifications.
- *Bred by Exhibitor Class:* Dogs older than six months bred and shown by the owner or member of the immediate family.
- *American Bred Class:* Dogs older than six months, bred and whelped in the United States.

• *Open Class:* Dogs older than six months; may be from foreign countries or even may be former Champions.

Step Two—Winner's Class

If your dog (male) or your bitch (female) wins in any one of the five classes it is eligible to compete in one of the Winner's Classes. Remember that there are two Winner's Classes, one for dogs and one for bitches, and only the winner of the Winner's Class (one dog and one bitch) will receive points.

Step Three—Best of Breed

Competition in the Winner's Class is fierce. It is composed not only of the day's winners, but the class is open to dogs (both male and female) that already have earned their championship points. This is the first time these beautiful, experienced dogs have been in the ring all day. Their handlers, who often spent their morning at the grooming tables in shorts or blue jeans, appear in spotlessly fresh outfits, with shoes shined and dog hairs brushed off. Exhibitors already out of the running, who may have been tending their own dogs or packing their cars, pause in their activities to watch the parade: these are the dogs from whom the next champions will come; these are the handlers who have learned the game. The winning dog or bitch will be named the show's Best of Breed.

Step Four—Best of Winners

Once the Best of Breed is selected from the Winner's Class, the judge has another decision to make. The two Winner's Class dogs (Winner's Dog and Winner's Bitch) must compete against each other for Best of Winners. (Of course, the day's Winner's Dog or Winner's Bitch could already have won the Best of Breed competition described in Step Three. This victory automatically makes that dog Best of Winners.)

Step Five—Best in Show

There are seven recognized groups of dogs at AKC shows: Sporting Group, Hound Group, Working Group, Terrier Group, Toy Group, Non-Sporting Group, and Herding Group. At an all-breed show like Westminster the first-place winner of each group enters the ring. The seven dogs representing seven different breeds, one from each group, compete against each other. At Westminster in February, 1993, the winning breeds in addition to Robert who represented the Sporting Group, were a borzoi, a komondor, a Dandie Dinmont terrier, a Pekingese, a bichon frise, and a German shepherd. Against this magnificent grouping, Robert (Ch. Salilyn's Condor), an English springer spaniel, won Best in Show.

Fun Matches

Don't be intimidated. If you think your Sandy is a winning example of springers, and you have time to indulge in the hobby of dog shows, step right in. Begin Sandy's show business career by entering a neighborhood fun match, usually sponsored by a local all-breed club. There you will meet other owners with similar interests, perhaps others with springers with whom you can trade tips.

Begin the day before by giving your springer a good brushing or a full bath. Remove any ticks or burrs, comb those silky ears, and trim any loose and obviously out of place hair. Stick a couple of doggy treats in your pocket, get there early (on-leash) and have a good time.

If, afterward, you decide you and Sandy both enjoyed the show, you may be hooked. If so, find a training class, find a grooming parlor or a good book, or maybe all three. You have lots to learn.

Sanctioned Matches

Sanctioned matches are those approved and announced by the AKC. These matches are held at stadiums, in gymnasiums, schools, and fair-grounds across the country. Contact your local all-breed club or your local springer club for information on matches near you. If you are new in town, call a veterinarian for advice. Usually one or several members of the staff attend and show at these matches and will welcome another member.

Obedience: Training Your Springer to Obey

Your springer's outlook on life, its confidence, and your relationship together is shaped by the way you handle its training. Every dog should learn the five basic disciplines: sit, stay, down, come, and heel. These basics were discussed under Puppy Kindergarten (see pages 53–57). Those owners who wish to go further with their pets should consider the AKC Obedience Trials which are divided into three areas of competence: Novice (Companion Dog), Open (Companion Dog Excellent), and Utility (Utility Dog).

The regulations are detailed in an American Kennel Club booklet available from their offices. The booklet explains the obedience trials, eligibility requirements, and locations of future events.

The United Kennel Club also hosts obedience trials which vary somewhat from the AKC requirements shown below. Both AKC- and UKC-earned obedience titles are placed in front of the dog's name on its pedigree.

Details on upcoming trials, qualifications, and registration information may be obtained from the United Kennel Club.

Teaching Advanced Obedience

Nothing can take the place of an experienced teacher and a classroom atmosphere. Some owners turn their dogs over to professional trainers skilled in coercing the most reluctant candidate to learn. This often involves boarding the dog with a trainer for a considerable amount of time. If you are interested, your local veterinarian can point you in the direction of a respected obedience trainer.

If you wish to train your own dog, books and videos can help, and there are a number of very good books on obedience training, some of which are listed in the back of this book, but there is no substitute for classes under an experienced trainer. Make a reservation for group training seminars often conducted by all-breed clubs following their Puppy Kindergarten basic obedience classes.

Advanced obedience training generally follows the AKC regulations for proficiency in the already mentioned levels of competition—that is, Novice, Open, and Utility.

Novice (C.D.): Dogs working on the novice degree of Companion Dog (C.D.), must learn six exercises: to heel on-leash, stand for examination, heel off-leash, come when called, sit for one minute, and stay down for three minutes.

Open (C.D.X.): Open class, Companion Dog Excellent (C.D.X.), is for dogs that have already earned the title of Companion Dog. To earn the C.D.X. degree each dog must be able to perform seven exercises: to heel off-leash, to drop on command, to sit for three minutes, to stay down for five minutes, to broad jump, and to perform two retrieves including one retrieve over a high jump. Some of these skills must be performed out of sight of the handler.

Utility (U.D.): The title of Utility Dog (U.D.), for dogs that have earned the C.D.X. degree, adds the challenges of hand-signal exercises, two scent discrimination tests, directed retrieves wherein the dog retrieves only specifically requested items, directed jumping tests, and a group examination.

Tracking (T.D., T.D.X.): Additionally, there are two AKC tracking titles, Tracking Dog (T.D.) and Tracking Dog Excellent (T.D.X.) that reward hard work and hard-won skills. The dogs must follow a scent laid three or more hours earlier over a course stretching perhaps 1,000 yards. The T.D.X. event is additionally complicated by having two people, strangers to the dog, cross the track to further test the dog's scent discrimination in trailing.

By the time you need information on this level of tracking you and your dog will have traveled a long way down the road of obedience and will have access to the latest rules concerning these abilities. You will also have learned that possession of these titles and others confers a great deal of respect on both dog and owner.

Field Work: Training Your Springer to Hunt

At least twenty million hunting licenses are sold each year. Many of these licenses are held by gamebird enthusiasts hunting with dogs. The springer is one of the top hunting partners for those interested in pheasant, quail, or waterfowl.

Even if you are not interested in hunting wild game, you and your springer would enjoy attending and perhaps participating in one of the forty or so AKC-licensed English Springer Spaniel Field Trials held each year.

Safety First

In these gun-conscious times, it should not be necessary to elaborate on the responsibility involved in working with a loaded shotgun. In a serious effort to reduce hunting accidents, many states require all first-time licensees to successfully complete a classroom firearm safety course with strong emphasis on wildlife conservation. Furthermore, most states require that hunters wear a hunter- orange jacket and cap when in a hunting area.

Responsible hunters can learn the basics of gun safety from public programs, from trained sports-

In early morning, both springer and camera are ready for the hunt.

men, and from informed sportsmen. All experts agree on the following minimal safety guidelines:
1. Unload your gun and keep it in its case until you arrive at the hunting area.
2. When walking, learn to carry your gun upside down on your shoulder (barrel pointed behind you and up.)
3. Treat every gun as if it were loaded. If someone asks, for instance, if a certain gun is loaded, say, "handle it as if it is."

Qualities to Look for in a Hunting Dog

Trainer Charles Goodall once wrote that "the selection of a gundog puppy slightly resembles forecasting the weather." Even so, and recognizing that all dogs love the spirit of the hunt, the presence or absence of certain qualities in a puppy can help assure you of a better candidate. Some top handlers have three suggestions to offer:
• Purchase your new puppy from field stock and not show stock. Field dogs have been bred for their size, their intelligence, and their enthusiasm for the hunt. The field fancy expects these

"birdier" puppies to be more intense in their enjoyment and in their skills.

- Choose the bold puppy, not the shy, clinging one. The aggressive puppy already chasing and retrieving leaves and sticks can be expected to enjoy the game of hunting.
- Avoid the puppy that jumps at loud noises. The dog must be trained to search in front of the hunter but always within shotgun range of no more than 50 to 60 yards (46–55 m).

Training the Hunting Puppy

By the time your puppy is three months old it can learn to retrieve a variety of items. A knotted sock makes a handy retrieve. Small items such as empty shotgun shells or stuffed toys with ornamental feathers added can be fun for your dog to retrieve. Some hunters prefer to begin their puppy training with a retrieving buck, a rolled canvas cylinder constructed like a small boat bumper. These and similar items are available at sporting goods shops.

You can begin with a knotted sock retrieve. Play with the puppy, dangling the sock in front of its nose, then toss it a short distance away. A good springer will always run after the sock. The dog may pick up the retrieve, perhaps shaking it and playing with it for awhile; sometimes your dog will carry it off to chew on it, but he will always run after it. That's not the problem. Your job is to get the puppy to return the sock to you.

Clap your hands, point to the sock, say "Sandy, Fetch!" Show some excitement. Put some enthusiasm in your body language. If Sandy starts to run away with the sock, back up and call him to you. Don't chase him. When you do get the sock back, call for Sandy's attention and toss it once more. Do this three or four times, no more. Quit while Sandy is still enjoying the game. Then, allow him to keep the sock. Later on, when the puppy loses interest in the sock, pick it up and put it away. Play the same game the next day.

If you have any trouble getting your puppy to come back to you, invest in a lightweight cord, about 10 to 15 feet (3–5 m) long. Attach the cord to the puppy's collar. You can't haul a reluctant dog in with this cord, but that isn't the point anyhow. You can gently guide your puppy to return to you by vocally encouraging him as well as softly tugging on the line. If Sandy drops the sock or object, encourage him to pick it up again. You shouldn't have much trouble teaching a good little springer to retrieve. Nature is working with you.

If Sandy comes in but won't release the sock, don't try to pull it from his mouth. He will only grip down harder and you don't want a hard-mouth springer. Try one of three proven techniques to get your dog to release. Say "drop," (or "give,") while

1. Taking his lower jaw in your hand, and pressing its lips lightly against his teeth.
2. Extending your middle finger and lightly striking the top of his nose.
3. Blowing short puffs of air onto his nose.

As the puppy ages and his jaw widens, this play-fetch can be varied by substituting other items such as the canvas buck mentioned earlier. Trainers suggest that by the time the puppy is three months old and you have been playing at hunt-retrieve with good results, add more noise to your routine. You have been clapping your hands whenever you sent the puppy out, now try shooting off a cap pistol. The idea is that eventually your puppy will look for a retrieve every time it hears a gunshot.

Many of the early obedience commands are also invaluable for hunting dog training. Depending on your intentions, to hunt or to demonstrate in obedience, you might substitute the hunting command "Hup" for the more common in obedience, "Sit."

A day in the field with a good dog can be a source of the purest pleasure you and your dog will ever share. The crisp fall afternoons with your springer at your side working hard at what it does best, will provide a lifetime of extraordinarily visual memories.

Keeping Your Springer Healthy

Your veterinarian will encourage you, as your pet's first line of defense, to be observant. You often will spot changes in behavior, eating habits, and activity levels before such abnormalities are apparent to others. Be aware. If your springer normally eats well, is frisky and playful one day and the next day it seems listless, refuses food, or feels warm, for instance, you should be alert for trouble. If this unusual behavior continues for several days, or is accompanied by a personality change, obvious intestinal problems, or hair loss, seek professional help.

You will be asked several questions. Be prepared with the answers.
• Are your pet's vaccinations complete and current?
• Have you made a recent change in your pet's diet?
• Is there an ongoing parasite control program?
• Have you noticed a marked decrease (or increase) in appetite, activity, or body temperature?
• Do you have any suspicions as to the cause?

Your Pet and the Veterinarian

Free bulletins and brochures are available from your veterinarian covering every subject from housetraining a new puppy to caring for an aging pet. Your veterinarian will be happy to share the latest research findings that will help keep your springer happy and healthy well into advanced old age.

Preventive Medicine

Your veterinarian has access to vaccines and preventive treatments designed to build up your pet's natural immunity. Failure to take advantage of these health enhancing regimes is unfair to your pet and often, as in the case of rabies vaccinations, illegal as well.

Your dog's veterinarian will be its second best friend.

Vaccines help prevent deadly and debilitating illnesses that can spread quickly through a neighborhood if left unchecked. Usually underway by the time a puppy is six weeks old and continued until age sixteen weeks, the following vaccines commonly are known as puppy shots. No pet should be without them.

Follow your veterinarian's lead on types and frequency of vaccines. Much depends on the area in which you live, the season, and recent disease occurrences in your community. A typical puppy schedule that provides up-to-date protection against the major diseases is as follows:
• Age six weeks—distemper-measles, parainfluenza, hepatitis, parvo, and corona
• Age eight weeks—parvo, corona, and bordetella
• Age ten weeks—parvo, corona
• Age twelve weeks—distemper, hepatitis, parvo, and initial heartworm preventive
• Age sixteen weeks—distemper, parainfluenza, parvo, hepatitis, and rabies.

Canine Distemper
Canine distemper, which at first resembles a common cold, is a highly contagious disease most

common in unvaccinated puppies during their first year of life. Distemper is the leading cause of infectious death in dogs. Consequently, most puppies are given their first distemper vaccination while still with their mother.

Symptoms of distemper include a watery discharge from the eyes (beginning as a thin fluid but in a few days turning to a thick, yellow consistency) and a dry, mucus-caked nose. The dog has a fever, shows loss of appetite, and is listless. By the time the dog evidences the typical epileptic-type seizures, treatment is ineffective.

Canine Hepatitis

An infectious disease that can spread to other dogs, canine hepatitis affects the liver, kidneys, and lining of the blood vessels.

In fatal form, the dog suddenly becomes ill showing symptoms of sudden pain and evidencing severe bloody diarrhea.

Kennel Cough

Kennel cough is a highly contagious disease that spreads rapidly through a group of dogs. The viruses and bacteria that cause kennel cough are repressed by the parainfluenza-Bordetella vaccine. Administered as part of an annual vaccination series, this vaccine is important for dogs living in groups and those that are exposed to others in show or hunting environments. Those infected, though seemingly cured, can later experience the aftereffect of chronic bronchitis.

Parvoviral Disease

Canine parvoviral disease is a relatively recent highly contagious disease first observed in the United States in 1978. The virus is transmitted from one dog to another through contaminated urine and feces. The usual victims are puppies under the age of five months. Springers, as well as rottweilers and dobermans are more likely than other breeds to develop severe complications if infected, making vaccination a must for these breeds.

Symptoms of parvoviral disease include depression, loss of appetite, vomiting, extreme pain, bloody diarrhea, and high fever. A second form of the disease seems to affect the puppy's heart muscles. An infected puppy will stop nursing, cry out, and gasp for breath. Death follows soon after.

Canine Coronaviral Gastroenteritis

This disease is characterized by the sudden onset of vomiting and persistent diarrhea. Although mortality rates for coronavirus are low, it is imperative that the coronavirus vaccine be included in the vaccination program for maximum immunity benefits.

Rabies

The rabies virus, deadly scourge of summer months, attacks its victim's brain. Rabies affects all warm-blooded animals, including fox, skunk, bat, and man. In some cases saliva can be infectious a week before any symptoms appear. A series of treatments has been developed for humans but rabies is fatal to dogs.

If you should encounter an animal that you suspect is rabid, keep your distance and call the authorities. Don't kill the animal. Laboratory tests on a dead animal can be misleading.

Heartworm Preventives

Heartworms have been identified in all fifty states, but many parts of the country, particularly those southern and western states with hot, long summers, are prime breeding grounds. The mosquito-borne larvae burrow their way into the dog's system. Once established, a female heartworm can produce ten thousand young every 24 hours.

Symptoms of heartworm infection include an intolerance for exercise and a soft, dry cough. Although mild cases of heartworms can be successfully treated, the best treatment is prevention.

Keeping Your Springer Healthy

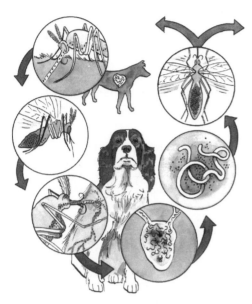

Heartworm infection begins when an infective mosquito deposits larvae on the dog's skin. Once she has burrowed into the dog's heart, a female heartworm can produce 10,000 young every 24 hours.

Heartworm preventives in monthly or daily doses, are vital for dogs in infested areas. The monthly dose can include, depending on the product, a preventive for roundworms, hookworms, and whipworms, making a year-round program invaluable.

How You Can Help

You are your dog's best friend. Be observant of its appetite, its elimination schedules, its moods. Inspect it for fleas and ticks and take appropriate measures to eradicate them. Stay in touch with your veterinarian and discuss deviations from the norm before such deviations get out of hand. Your pet depends on you for its health.

Taking Your Springer's Temperature

You should know your dog's normal body temperature. A hand held to the dog's nose is not always as reliable as is commonly believed. Although a cold, wet nose is one sign of good health, a dry nose is not in itself a sign of illness.

Your veterinarian will take your healthy pet's temperature during routine puppy-shot visits. Note the range. A healthy springer usually registers around 101 degrees F (38.3 degrees C).

Obtain a heavy-duty rectal thermometer. Shake it down to at least the 96 degrees F (35.5 degrees C) mark. Lubricate it well. Lift your dog's tail, and using a twisting motion, insert two-thirds of the thermometer into the anal canal. Remove, wipe clean, and read. A reading more than 2 degrees Farenheit (1 degree Celsius) above normal is considered too high.

Giving Medicine

Eventually, every pet owner must learn to administer medicine, vitamin supplements, or heartworm preventive. Some medications, such as

C'mon now, open up. It's good for you.

Keeping Your Springer Healthy

Hold the dog's mouth closed and stroke its throat until it swallows.

the heartworm preventives, are apparently pretty tasty. Take advantage of this unexpected benefit when you can because some medicines seem to be pretty obnoxious.

The accepted procedure is to open your pet's mouth and place the pill at the back of the tongue. Hold the mouth shut and stroke the dog's throat. When you release your hand, if the dog licks its nose, it has swallowed the pill.

You might, however, take advantage of your dog's impulse to swallow its food whole. Tear off two small bits of cheese. Place the pill in one piece and roll both pieces into a ball. Call the dog to you. Command it to "sit!" and offer the plain cheese ball first. Then offer the cheese-wrapped pill. Occasionally, vary the treat either by offering the cheese-pill first, or coating the pill with peanut butter instead of cheese.

One veterinarian suggests cutting a Fig Newton in half, pushing the pill in one half and feeding it to your springer. The other half is for you.

The fact that a springer's jaw has loose skin between the teeth and the lip can be used to your advantage when offering liquid medication. Again, tell your dog to "sit!". Using your fingers, pull out the dog's lower lip at the back of its mouth, near the jaw hinge. Pour the medicine into this "pocket" allowing it to dribble down between the teeth into the dog's throat.

Weighing Your Springer

A simple procedure like getting your dog on a scale can sometimes be not so simple. Dogs dislike unsteady, shifting ground and the best dog will resist your best efforts. Your veterinarian is trained to out-maneuver your pet and has access to professional floor-scale equipment.

If you feel the need at home to know just how much weight Sandy has gained, you might try this: Step on the scale alone. Record your weight. Pick up your pet and step back on the scale. Make a note of the weight. Then, when you subtract the first figure from the second, the difference in the two figures is your dog's weight.

Some Common and Not So Common Problems

By the time your pet is six weeks old you should have established a good relationship with your veterinarian. Immunization schedules and behavior problems should be discussed and solutions agreed on. Your veterinarian will be pleased to help you maintain your pet's health between scheduled visits. Call if you need advice.

Fleas: Fleas and ticks are the bane of summer for our dogs. Unless we intervene, our pets scratch and bite their way through a miserable July and August until we and they are frantic. In our efforts to help, we throw an avalanche of products at the flea: chemically treated collars, ultrasonic collars, medicated shampoos and dips, chemical spot-infusions, garlic, brewer's yeast, and herbal medications. The house is quiet for awhile, our pet is comfortable but all too soon the scratch is on again. What has happened?

In order to treat these pesty critters successfully it is important to understand their life cycle.

A flea's life cycle consists of four stages: egg, larva, pupa, and adult. Your pest control efforts must seek out and demolish the flea at each stage or you have only temporarily delayed the cycle, not eliminated it.

Adult fleas live by feeding on blood. Once the flea has fed, it must continue taking regular blood feedings or it will die. If it leaves the host for any length of time it cannot survive. You can kill adult fleas with dips and powders. Your dog can literally scratch them off its body, but the problem is that the adult flea began producing eggs within two to three days after receiving the first blood meal. The flea can produce 40 to 50 eggs per day at its peak production, a rate that can continue for several months, and produce several hundred eggs over the insect's lifespan of six to twelve months. So, the fleas you killed today with an insecticidal dip were only 1 percent of the potential number of fleas in your dog's environment. A point to remember: For every flea you see, one hundred more are in various stages of development or in hiding.

Once laid, the flea's tiny, white, oval eggs probably fell off your pet and landed on your sofa cushions, in its bedding, on your carpets, or in the yard. Two to twelve days later these eggs hatched into small, maggotlike larvae. The larvae formed pupae (cocoons) from which eventually emerged—you guessed it—adult fleas, hungry for a blood meal.

The secret to flea control, therefore, is to treat the flea's environment at each of its four stages of development. Ask your veterinarian to recommend a product for your area and be prepared for a four-week eradication schedule.

Week one: Wash your dog's bed. Vacuum the carpet, the furniture, and the drapes. When you

Tapeworms, transmitted by fleas, live in the small intestine. Body segments, which resemble grains of rice, often are observed in the dog's stool.

are finished vacuuming, change vacuum bags. Burn or otherwise dispose of the old bag. Sprinkle or spray the recommended product around your dog's sleeping quarters and play yard. Shampoo your pet with a good flea shampoo. Pay particular attention to the dog's head, under its arms, and its anus.

Week two: Wash your dog's bed. Vacuum as before. Don't forget to burn or otherwise dispose of the old bag. If you don't, fleas will hatch in the bag. Use the insecticide as recommended.

Week three: Follow the same procedure as week one. Your dog will receive two shampoos during this four-week assault (weeks one and three). Make bathing times fun for the dog.

Week four: Wash, vacuum, and spray as before. Be assured that although this program is initially time consuming it is effective for weeks even months provided no reinfestation is introduced. Unfortunately, you must be prepared to resume treatment at the first sign of an outbreak.

Ticks: If your dog spends a lot of time outside, you should schedule a thorough, daily tick inspection. Although all ticks are capable of transmitting disease, the deer tick in eastern and midwestern states and the Pacific coast tick found in Washington, Oregon, and California, cause the most problems. Lyme disease, named in 1975 for the Connecticut community that first brought it to our attention, is potentially fatal to humans.

Ticks attach to your dog to feed and mate. The female will settle anywhere on your dog, usually on its ear flaps, around its neck, or between its toes, sometimes gorging until it is the size of a large gray pea. To remove the tick, douse it with an alcohol-drenched cotton swab. She should die within five or six minutes. Then, using tweezers, catch the tick as close to the dog's body as possible and pull steadily. When the tick is removed examine it to be sure the head was released intact. If the head is torn, go back and look for mouthparts that may not have been removed. Swab the spot with more alcohol, search for and remove the smaller male tick which should be resting nearby.

Mange: Usually characterized by excessive hair loss, mange is caused by mites that live in the pores of the dog's skin, burrowing into the skin to lay eggs. There are two types of mange, demodectic and sarcoptic. Dogs with sarcoptic mange scratch and itch excessively. The ear tips are often affected; in fact, crusty ear tips and a musty body odor are prime symptoms. Sarcoptic mange is treated with an insecticidal dip.

Veterinarians suspect that the demodectic mange, usually seen in puppies three to nine months old, is caused by a lack of immune response that may be hereditary. The Demodex canis mite is present in many dogs but causes problems only for a few. Some untreated puppies make spontaneous recoveries as their immune systems mature. However, the difficulties of adolescence, a change in habits, or a move to a new location can bring on an attack. The disease is characterized by hair loss from the front legs and face of affected puppies. As it progresses, the hair loss becomes generalized over the entire body. Unlike sarcoptic mange, demodectic mange does not itch.

Allergies and Hot Spots: Dogs have allergies just as people do. A dog can be allergic to almost anything, sneezing and itching in response to seasonal cycles, its environment, or occasional unfortunate contacts. Allergies also may cause the painful, itching, weeping bare patches of skin known as hot spots.

If your dog itches and sneezes consider some of these most common causes:

• contact allergens such as insecticides, detergents, soaps, flea powders, flea collars, plastic or rubber food dishes, or outdoor carpet dyes;
• food allergens such as soy, beef, chicken, corn, wheat, egg whites, milk, and fish;
• inhaled allergens such as house dust, ragweed, tree pollens, wool, feathers, and molds.

Your veterinarian can identify some of these causes by means of allergy testing and allergy shots. In addition, your veterinarian can suggest the proper hypoallergenic diet if necessary and can prescribe ointments and diet additives, many of which contain such anti-inflammatory agents as omega 3 and omega 6 that reduce itching by as much as 20 percent.

Worms: Most puppies are born with roundworms. Conscientious breeders deworm each litter at two or three weeks of age and again at five or six weeks. Many adult dogs are subject to whipworms, hookworms, and tapeworms. Although the puppies develop a certain immunity once treated, some rural owners routinely deworm their adults dogs once a year.

Diarrhea and Vomiting: Debilitating to the dog and unpleasant for the owner, continuing, foul-smelling diarrhea is a problem that should be treated immediately. Occasional diarrhea can be caused by indiscreet eating. Garbage, milk, rich food, a change in diet, or toxic plants often have a laxative effect. A rule of thumb is, if your dog throws up once or twice or if it has an occasional soft stool, it probably is all right. Cut back on its food and offer only dry kibble until the problem clears. If vomiting or diarrhea persist, however, call your veterinarian.

Hereditary Problems: The typical English springer matures into a well-adjusted, amiable, confident companion comfortable in its reputation as a healthy, genetically reliable breed. As with all breeds, however, the springer has its share of inherited problems.

One problem in particular, the dog's sudden, uncontrolled aggression, is commonly referred to as Rage syndrome. The springer is one of several breeds in which the disorder has been recognized. Animal behaviorist Karen Overall, speaking before the Morris Animal Foundation, identified the typical "toggle-switch, on/off" behavior characterizing this aggression. "The dog will be uncontrollably aggressive—you could hit it over the head with a two-by-four and it wouldn't notice you were there," said Ms. Overall, a lecturer at Pennsylvania School of Veterinary Medicine, "and then it turns off just as suddenly."

The syndrome, diagnosed in the early 1970s, has caused springer breeders to intensify recognition and identification of suspected carrier lines. A survey designed by a local springer club temperament committee and mailed to members of the ESSFTA, asked owners to assess their former and present pets' reaction to discipline, their behavior and temperament as well as their hyperactivity, aggression, or possessiveness. When tabulated, results will provide breeders with data to evaluate springer temperament and to identify afflicted dogs.

Ms. Overall noted that although the disorder is "probably overdiagnosed and under-reported," she warned her audience that animals afflicted with this syndrome are "extremely, extremely dangerous." If you have reason to suspect your dog's behavior, contact your veterinarian immediately.

Although fewer than 20 percent of English springers tested by the Orthopedic Foundation for Animals evidenced genetically generated hip problems, some lines do carry a defective gene for dysplastic hips and elbows that if untreated cause great discomfort to the dog. Symptoms of dysplasia begin to show at about six months of age.

Some lines carry the defective genes that cause PRA (progressive retinal atrophy, an eye problem that can lead to blindness), cutaneous asthenia (a connective tissue problem), fucosidosis (a neurological disease), and PFK (a hereditary enzyme deficiency of the blood). Ask your breeder and double-check with your veterinarian.

Emergencies

All pet owners should be aware of certain procedures that could make the difference between life and death of their pet. Primary among these are the sudden illnesses and traumas of poisons and fractures.

A strategically located home first aid kit for your pet will help you in the event of an emergency.
• tweezers
• scissors
• rubbing alcohol
• moist towelettes
• cotton-tipped swabs
• 3-inch (7.6 cm) roller gauze
• 3 × 3-inch (7.6 cm) sterile gauze pads
• rectal thermometer
• hydrogen peroxide

Bleeding and Fractures: A broken leg is the most common fracture and one that must be handled with great care until professional help is available. Try to keep the dog calm. Your primary responsibility is to immobilize the affected limb. Try not to move the dog until you can get a splint on the fracture. Bone grinding against muscle and tissue can be excruciating, so work carefully. First, muzzle the dog to prevent injury to the handler. Then, straighten the leg as much as

Keeping Your Springer Healthy

Trained specialists carefully move an injured springer.

you can. Use whatever is at hand—a yardstick, broom handle, rolled up magazine—to immobilize the limb. Wrap the splint with gauze, torn strips of cotton, or a necktie before transporting the dog to a veterinarian.

Poisoning, Bites, and Stings: Puppies are inquisitive creatures, biting and snapping randomly at insects, lizards, and assorted flying hazards. Although older dogs have learned through sad experience to keep away from wasps, snakes, and the like, the urge to snap at that annoying sound is occasionally too much to resist. Likewise, the sweet taste of antifreeze, the aroma of arsenic in snail and slug bait, and the appealing odor of decayed food are sometimes irresistible. Cocoa hull, often sold as garden mulch, contains theobromine which is toxic to dogs.

Here are some common items that can cause problems for your springer if imbibed in sufficient quantities:
- chocolate
- onions
- "people" medicine (antihistamines, sleeping pills, blood pressure pills)
- house plants (Japanese yew, diffenbachia, philodendron, poinsettia, chrysanthemums, pothos)

- outdoor shrubs (rhododendrons, oleanders, azaleas, wild cherry)
- zinc (from pennies or from the nuts and bolts of kennel crates)

The following rank among the deadliest combinations hazardous to your pet:
- rat poisons containing strychnine, sodium fluroacetate or warfarin (the dead rodent itself is poisonous);
- phosphorous found in fireworks or matches;
- corrosives in household cleaners;
- fumes from gasoline, kerosene, and turpentine;
- antifreeze in doses of ½ teaspoonful per pound of bodyweight;
- lead from paint, plaster, and putty.

Although the majority of snakes are non-poisonous and their bites non-fatal, all snakebites can be extremely painful. Because snakebites from one of the poisonous varieties can be treated with specific antivenins, it is important to kill and identify the snake.

Some of the symptoms of poisoning are abdominal pain, panting, vomiting, excessive drooling, tremors, uncoordinated gait, convulsions, and coma. If you suspect your dog has been poisoned, call your veterinarian immediately. If you are

The dog's leash can be used as a temporary muzzle.

unable to reach your veterinarian, or need further information on the toxicity of specific substances, call the National Animal Poison Control Center at 1-900-680-0000. The Center, opened in 1978 as a service of the University of Illinois, is staffed by health professionals who will answer your questions and make specific recommendations for your situation.

The Older Springer

After the first few years of rambunctious puppyhood and rebellious adolesence, you and your dog will come to know each other well. Your springer will hear your car long before it turns into the driveway; it will distinguish your step from all the others it hears, and it will seem to read your thoughts—especially when outings and food are involved. You will settle into comfortable habits, your friendship the dearer with age. With good care and good luck our springer companions will live with us for 12 or more years.

Life Expectancy

As a result of a series of studies on life expectancy experts have revised their approximations of equivalent ages of dog and human. The old one-for-seven equivalency is no more: At one time we believed that a one-year-old dog was the same physical and mental age as a seven-year-old child, for instance, but later studies lead us to believe a one-year-old dog is more equivalent to a 15-year-old adolescent.

Euthanasia: By the time your springer is ten years old you will notice a change in its daily routines. It will nap more frequently, chase butterflies less often, be slower to rise, and less flexible in its movements. As it ages, hardening of the arteries puts a burden on its heart. Cancer, heart disease, and kidney disease are its enemies. Its coat will thin out and damaged hair will regrow at a slower rate. It will be less surefooted and will not attempt

Dog/Human Age Equivalents

Dog's Age	Human's Age
6 months	10 years
8 months	13 years
10 months	14 years
1 year	15 years
18 months	20 years
2 years	24 years
4 years	32 years
6 years	40 years
8 years	48 years
10 years	56 years
12 years	64 years
14 years	72 years
16 years	80 years
18 years	88 years
20 years	96 years
21 years	100 years

climbs it once made so easily. You can help your old friend by following a few, simple rules:
• Feed it a diet with higher protein, lower fat, and higher fiber to discourage obesity.
• Encourage moderate amounts of daily exercise to help its joints remain flexible.
• Don't change its daily routine. Avoid unnecessary travel and unfamiliar sleeping arrangements.
• Don't let your pet loose near traffic; hearing goes before sight and smell.
• Consider allowing it to leave this life with dignity.

Often, an old dog, beset with age-related ill health can find no relief from suffering. It is then time to say good-bye. Your veterinarian will know when that time has come. Modern drugs can help that end come swiftly and without pain.

In her novel, *The Flowering*, Agnes Sligh Turnbull spoke for many: "Dogs' lives are too short. Their only fault, really."

Breeding Your Springer

Once that delightful puppy has matured you will find that it requires a different kind of attention. Those dependent puppy days are over. No more worrying about getting up in the middle of the night to let it out; your puppy's bladder is under control. No more uncertainty when an automobile drives past the house; your springer's enthusiasm is under control. No more wondering if your puppy will come when called; you are in control.

The two of you can go for long companionable walks. You understand each other. There never has been a better dog. A beautiful disposition, a shining coat—what more could you want from a pet? Perhaps puppies; another pet just like this one?

Do neighbors ask for you to save them a puppy if you plan to breed? Do strangers comment on your springer, admiring its color, its handsome head, its carriage? Do you think the world needs six more springers just like yours? Then, by all means, this chapter is for you.

If, on the other hand, your springer's attitude needs an adjustment, its coat hasn't recovered from that last demodectic mange attack, and you don't really have the energy after caring for your family to take on a litter of puppies, this chapter is also for you. Let's take the last first.

Spaying and Neutering

If you have decided that the springer world is already well supplied with puppies you should consider spaying or neutering your pet. Female puppies can be spayed at any time after six months of age. It is not necessary for her health that she have a litter first. Spaying is a simple surgical procedure that will, in addition to preventing her from having puppies, reduce the chance of mammary tumors and, of course, eliminate the possibility of uterine or ovarian cancer. Spaying will not alter her personality.

Neutering is a surgical procedure performed on male dogs that involves removal of both testicles. Because castration, as the procedure is called, can affect the male's secondary sex characteristics, it is best performed at about one year of age. Neutering is often performed on aggressive dogs, and on those who wander far from their home territory in search of females in heat.

Choosing a Mate

Mating two dogs is a science that involves record keeping, observation, and study. The science of genetics enables us to predict possible results from a particular breeding. The most important point for us to remember at this time is that genetics has no use for averages. Suppose, for instance, that your female has perfect temperament and outstanding coat coloration. Her problem is that her ears could be a little longer and could be set a little lower on her head. You will not improve her line one bit by mating her to a dog with exceptionally long, low-set ears.

Each dog has more than 25,000 genes carried on 39 pairs of chromosomes. One gene in each pair comes from each parent, so every puppy receives approximately 50 percent of its genes from the male and 50 percent from the female. Within each pair, one gene is usually dominant. The dominant gene is the gene that shows: long ears or color, for instance. Our mythical puppy may receive long ears from its father, but recessively retain his mother's gene for high ear-set. Thus, recessive genes do not disappear. They wait until a second mating, when if matched by another recessive gene of the same type, the traits will emerge. These can be coat color, eye color, hip deformities, or others.

Because the genetic possibilities of inheritance are almost infinite, accurate record keeping and intensive study of bloodlines are very important breeding tools.

Breeding Your Springer

Breeding Systems

Three factors influence our choice of breeding partners for our pets, but two of them are less likely to produce that perfect litter we all hope for.

Outcrossing is breeding two dogs that have no common ancestor over the last five or six generations. This choice, often used by backyard breeders, can produce beautiful puppies or can produce sorry specimens of the breed. Outcrossing should be accompanied by specific record keeping, analysis, and observation.

Inbreeding, the mating of two immediate relatives, (brother to sister, mother to son, daughter to father) is a gamble best not attempted by the amateur. Each puppy will receive twice as many of both desirable and undesirable genes.

Linebreeding is the surest path to take when breeding two quality dogs: Grandfather to granddaughter, uncle to niece, cousin to cousin, for instance, are acceptable and desirable linebreeding tactics. This quality to quality genetic pairing yields consistently good puppies, some with superior qualities.

Preparation for Breeding

The professional breeder will not mate the most genetically compatible dogs unless both dogs meet the following requirements:
• current vaccinations including those for Bordetella bacterium and coronavirus;
• clear of parasites and heartworms;
• tested for canine brucellosis;
• hips and elbows tested OFA good or better;
• male at least one year old; female at least eighteen months old and in at least her second heat;
• neither dog older than seven years.

In addition, the owner of the female needs to make allowances for the following considerations:
• a list of prospective puppy homes;

• free owner time (at least an hour at a time, four times a day for two to three weeks);
• the added expense of additional food, veterinarian fees, vaccination costs and advertising;
• record keeping, reading, and learning;
• a contingency plan if the litter does not sell in nine to ten weeks.

Presuming that you have come this far, welcome to the club! Expect to have an intense nine to ten weeks of learning about, cleaning up, playing with, and training springers.

The Practicalities

Although the male can evince interest at almost any time, the female is fertile only twice a year. This fertility period, called heat, begins when she is about seven to ten months of age and will continue every six months or thereabouts until she is seven or eight years old. The heat lasts for approximately 21 days. For only part of this time can she actually conceive. Failure to conceive is often a result of misunderstanding this cycle.
• The first six to nine days the vulva swells and she is attractive to male dogs but will not accept their advances.
• She will accept and on occasion aggressively seek the male between the tenth and sixteenth days of the cycle. She shows readiness by holding her tail aside and standing quietly.
• The last part of the cycle, from the seventeenth to twenty-first day, both parties lose interest.

Traditionally, the female is brought to the male. Nontraditionally, frozen sperm from top stud dogs makes artificial insemination a viable option. Both methods involve a fee paid to the owner of the male. Depending on the quality, conformation, and heritage of the line, that fee can be quite expensive, and is frequently based on a percentage of the eventual value of the litter. The fee is usually paid at the time of service. You might want to clarify in advance what will happen if the female does not conceive. Some

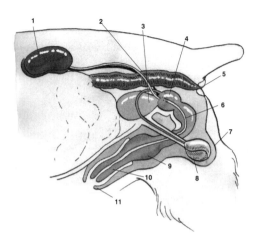

Male Internal Organs: 1. Kidney; 2. Rectum; 3. Bladder; 4. Prostate; 5. Anus; 6. Urethra; 7. Scrotum; 8. Testicles; 9. Bulb; 10. Penis; 11. Sheath.

stud dog owners will offer a second try, some will not.

Some stud owners will agree to a pick of the litter instead of a fee. In this case, the pick may be made early although the puppy will remain with its mother until at least seven weeks. Because no other buyer may select until after the pick is made, it is advantageous to the litter owner and the owner of the stud to agree on a pick-date so that others may be accommodated.

Although family, friends, and neighbors will visit the litter almost from day one, most litter owners find it best to set aside the day that the litter is seven weeks old for prospective owners to make a final selection. At that time, new owners may, one by one, set off with their new puppies to a new life.

The Mating Procedure
• Neither dog should be fed for at least two hours prior to the mating.

• Both owners should be present (in order to register the litter, the dam's owner must testify to the mating).
• Both animals should be on a leash.
• The owner of the female, or someone the dog feels comfortable with, should be at the female's head to prevent her from biting the stud dog.
• The male will mount the female from the rear, holding her loins with his legs while thrusting.
• The tie lasts between 10 and 45 minutes during which time the male will throw his leg over the female's back so they can stand more comfortably back to back.
• Never try to break the tie. The male's penis contains a bone that may break if enough pressure is applied. The female could be internally damaged.
• For insurance, and with a day of rest in between, a second mating usually takes place. The resulting litter, however, is dated as though pregnancy had occurred, as it probably did, during the first mating.

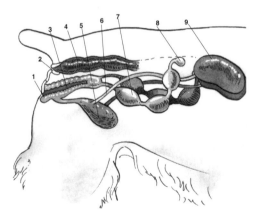

Female Internal Organs: 1. Vulva; 2. Anus; 3. Vagina; 4. Rectum; 5. Bladder; 6. Ureter; 7. Developing Embryo; 8. Ovaries; 9. Kidneys.

Breeding Your Springer

Pregnancy

If conception has occurred, the birth follows in 60 to 65 days (nine weeks). During this waiting period, continue to exercise your springer every day. Feed her normal diet for the first two or three weeks, gradually switching to a higher protein diet such as a puppy kibble. Make the food change over a period of at least four days, substituting first one-fourth, then one-half, then three-quarters of the high protein food. The fourth day feed 100 percent of the new, higher protein food.

As the puppies grow, they crowd the dam's stomach and she might prefer smaller, more frequent meals. Also, during weeks six to nine of her pregnancy her daily ration should be increased by half and divided into smaller meals as before.

The Whelping Box

At least two weeks before the expected due date you should prepare a bed for your pet, encouraging her to sleep in it if she will. The springer and her puppies will spend most of their time in the bed and thus will require sufficient space to stretch out in comfortably. A box 4 by 5 feet (1.2 × 1.5 m) allows space for a partition that will allow the dam some privacy later on. A large plastic wading pool works well as a one-time whelping box.

Whatever your choice, the interior must be easy to keep clean. Layer several sheets of newspaper on the bottom of the box. On top of the newspapers place heavy towels, an old mattress pad, a throw rug, or any other washable or disposable material.

After the whelping box has been set up, gather materials for a support box of your own. A sturdy cardboard box will hold your birthing supplies and will serve as an instant incubator later as well as a portable carrier for that first visit to the veterinarian. Line the bottom of the box with layers of newspaper. Cover the paper with an old towel.

Add the following items:
- heating pad or hot water bottle
- postal scale that will register up to two pounds
- notebook and pencil
- several packages of colored rick-rack or ribbon
- flashlight
- room thermometer
- clock
- infant nasal bulb syringe
- sterile gloves
- dental floss
- scissors
- iodine

Delivery

Watch your springer carefully the last few days. The first sign of labor is often the breaking of her water bag. The first sign for you might be the disappearance of your dog as she instinctively seeks a quiet place for delivery. On the other hand, your springer may follow your every step as she did when she was a puppy. If you don't accompany her to her box she will try to have her litter at your feet or under the kitchen table.

Make a note of the time. Alert your veterinarian. Bring out your support box. Empty the box of everything but the bottom soft layers and the heating pad. The bottom of the box should

Mother and babies are doing fine. Note the flared sides of the box that prevent the relaxing dam from smothering a member of her litter.

be warm, about 85 to 90 degrees F (29–32 degrees C).

The puppies should appear at regular intervals, from 15 minutes to an hour apart. Weigh and identify each puppy as it arrives. If sight identification is insufficient, colored rick-rack around the neck, a different color for each (although you can have a boy-yellow and a girl-yellow) simplifies the process. Place the newborns in your warmed support box while the mother is delivering successive members of the litter, returning them to her to nurse in between births.

Caring for Newborn Puppies

The puppies, encased in a membrane, are unable to breathe on their own. This membrane, the placenta, must be removed within thirty seconds after birth. As each puppy arrives the mother will lick and tear at the membrane, consuming it. Her rough tongue will stimulate the puppy, causing it to breathe and eliminate. Unless the dam ignores the puppy and in so doing fails to remove the placenta, do not interfere. Although such a possibility is rare, pain, confusion, or distraction could suppress a young mother's maternal instincts. If you must intervene, lift the puppy and hold it with a towel while you forcibly peel away the membrane; begin at the puppy's head. Use your bulb syringe to clear any secretions from its mouth. Again using the towel, briskly rub the puppy to stimulate it. As soon as possible, and if the mother will accept it, return the puppy to her. The dam will examine the puppy, lick it, and instinctively sever the umbilical cord by shredding it with her teeth. You should check the umbilical cord within a few hours for signs of bleeding. If necessary, the dental floss in your box can serve as a tourniquet to help close the cord.

The First Hours

Although Nature takes marvelous care of her little ones, some situations require your assistance. You should call your veterinarian when:

• the dam is in hard and serious labor for more than an hour without delivering a puppy;
• she passes dark green or bloody fluid before the birth of the first puppy (bloody fluid is not abnormal after the first puppy);
• a large puppy is visible in the vaginal opening, but it appears and disappears with each contraction;
• labor stops for more than an hour and the dam is restless, whimpering, or anxious.

What to Expect: Your springer will be tired after the delivery. She will want to rest and will want some quiet time with her new family. You may offer her a drink of cool water, which she will likely refuse. Let her rest and turn your attention to the puppies.

A puppy is born the same temperature as its mother. Because it has no internal thermostat and because its temperature drops rapidly after birth, cold is its greatest enemy. Keep the floor temperature of the whelping box between 85 degrees F (29 degrees C) to 90 degrees F (32 degrees C) for at least the first week. Then, reduce the temperature in the box five degrees Farenheit (three or less degrees Centigrade) each week for three weeks striving for a permanently comfortable 70 degrees F (21 degrees C).

Weigh each puppy 12 hours after birth and again at 24 hours. The majority of puppies, at 24 hours, will have gained weight. Record each puppy's weight weekly. Healthy puppies will double their birth weight in eight to ten days. Weight gain should be steady. Check the rick-rack regularly for fit.

The First Weeks

A newborn puppy comes into the world deaf and blind. It cannot urinate or defecate without help. It cannot walk. It sleeps in a curled position with its head tucked under its chest. In fact, until it is three weeks old, a puppy will sleep 90 percent of the time. As it will spend the remaining 10 percent of its time eating, and its mother will regularly clean up any resulting mess, your main responsibilities should be confined to record keeping and observation.

The puppy's eyes open at about two weeks and it can hear. Though wobbly, it can stand. At three weeks, still wobbly, it can walk.

Your puppies are most vulnerable the first four days of life. Ten percent of the puppies whelped do not survive the first two weeks of life. Of this 10 percent, 75 percent do not survive four days. Litter mortality can be caused by several factors. The dam may not have been fed properly during pregnancy. Her vaccinations may not have been current. The puppy may have been physically immature, or may have suffered a birth trauma. It could have had a congenital defect or a bacterial infection.

Sometimes, despite our best efforts, the cause of mortality is difficult to identify. An entire litter, apparently healthy at birth, regresses, and even with veterinary attention, one by one the puppies weaken and die. These puppies are classic examples of fading puppy syndrome.

Watch the mother carefully for signs of inadequate milk production, inattentiveness to her litter, or a change in disposition. Feed her regularly and allow her to exercise if she will. For the first three weeks, she should attend to her litter with only minimal help from you. She will feed them, clean up after them, and keep them warm.

Weaning: When, in three to four weeks, you notice she is spending less and less time with them, or is nursing standing up, escaping frequently, you should help her wean them by offering the puppies two meals a day of mashed puppy kibble softened in warm water or bitch's milk replacer. (Cow's milk is not suitable for puppies.)

Put the mother out of the room. (She will be glad for the vacation). Pour the mixture, which

A job well done: a healthy puppy ready and eager for a new world of companionship.

should be about the consistency of thick soup, into a large tray and set the tray on a bed of newspapers on the floor. Introduce the puppies, one at a time, to the new experience by dipping one finger into the mix and letting the puppy suck it clean. Some puppies, hungrier or more aggressive, will need no encouragement beyond a tentative nose-dip, and will stand four-square in the middle of the pan to feed. Some want none of the new, messy experience and will back off and go back to sleep. All will carry a mess back to the nest unless you clean them off first.

When the puppies have finished (or wandered off) allow the mother in to finish the meal and to finish cleaning up behind them. Gather the newspapers and clean the pan. Take a break. There will be another mealtime in four hours.

When the puppies are eating well, gradually decrease the amount of liquid while increasing feedings to four a day. As long as the mother is willing to spend the night with them and allow them to nurse, encourage her to do so.

Registering the Litter

Within a week of whelping, send the completed litter-registration application to the AKC or UKC following their instructions. You will receive a set of registration applications, one for each puppy, that will accompany the puppy to its new home. The new owners then apply for permanent registration in their name.

New Homes for Your Puppies

At seven weeks of age your puppies are ready for a life of their own away from the mother, away from the litter, away from you. Many articles have been written about the importance of choosing appropriate new homes for your precious litter. All agree that with care your puppies will be transferred to loving homes that will provide for them, nurturing and caring for them, as long as they live. You, of course, will ask these new adoptive owners to keep in touch with you and to call you at once if problems develop that need your help. You will offer to take back any puppy with congenital defects or those that inexplicably die. In later months, should the new family be unable to care for the puppy, or should the family move and be unable to take the puppy with them, you will want to be notified so you can place the puppy in another home.

Prepare a puppy kit containing photographs of early days, a copy of the pedigree, a small supply of puppy food, and an up-to-date medical record chart. Assure the new owners of your continued support and encourage them to call with questions. Kiss your babies good-bye and rest assured you have prepared them well to step confidently into the world of purebred dogs, friendly, healthy, and eager for the experience.

Just think, six more springers, just like yours!

Useful Literature and Addresses

Modern Sources

American Kennel Club. *The Complete Dog Book.* New York: Howell, 1985.

_____. *American Kennel Club Dog Care and Training.* New York: Howell, 1991.

Bashkim, Dibra, and Randolph, Elizabeth. *Dog Training by Bash.* New York: Signet, 1992.

Campbell, Richard. *Behavior Problems in Dogs.* Edited by Duane F. Warren. Santa Barbara, CA: American Veterinary Publications, 1975.

Gaines Professional Services. *Basic Guide to Canine Nutrition.* Edited by James H. Sokolowski, D.V.M., Ph.D., and Anthony M. Fletcher, D.V.M. Chicago: Gaines, 1987.

Goodall, Charles S. *How to Train Your Gun Dog.* New York: Howell, 1991.

Haddon, Cecilia. *Faithful to the End.* New York: St. Martins, 1991.

Haggerty, Capt. Arthur J., and Benjamin, Carol Lea. *Dog Tricks.* New York: Howell, 1978.

Kilcommons, Brian. *Good Owners, Great Dogs.* New York: Warner, 1992.

Monks of New Skete. *How to Be Your Dog's Best Friend, a Training Manual for Dog Owners.* Boston: Little, Brown, 1978.

_____. *The Art of Raising a Puppy.* Boston: Little, Brown, 1991.

Morris, Desmond. *Dog Watching.* New York: Crown, 1986.

Pfaffenberger, Clarence. *The New Knowledge of Dog Behavior.* New York: Howell, 1963.

Siegel, Mordecai, and Margolis, Matthew. *When Good Dogs Do Bad Things.* Boston: Little, Brown, 1986.

Taylor, David, B.V.M.S. *You and Your Dog.* With Peter Scott, M.R.C.V.S. New York: Knopf, 1991.

Ullman, Hans-J., and Ullman, Evamaria. *The New Dog Handbook.* Hauppauge, New York: Barron's Educational Series, Inc. 1985.

Winokur, Jon, ed. *Mondo Canine.* New York: Penguin, 1991.

Wolters, Richard A. *Gun Dog.* New York: Dutton, 1961.

_____. *Family Dog.* New York: Dutton, 1975.

_____. *Home Dog.* New York: Dutton, 1984.

Woodhouse, Barbara. *No Bad Dogs.* New York: Summit, 1982.

Wrede, Barbara. *Civilizing Your Puppy.* Hauppauge, New York: Barron's Educational Series, Inc., 1992.

English Springer Sources

Bush, Barbara. *Millie's Book.* New York: William Morrow, 1990.

Sanford, William R. and Green, Carl. *The English Springer Spaniel.* New York: Crestwood, 1989.

Ullman, Hans-J., and Ullman, Evamaria. *Spaniels, A Complete Pet Owner's Manual.* Hauppauge, New York: Barron's Educational Series, Inc., 1982.

Out-of-Print Sources

Lorenz, Konrad Z. *Man Meets Dog.* trans. Marjorie Kerr Wilson. Boston: Houghton Mifflin, 1955.

Maeterlinck, Maurice. *Our Friend the Dog.* Edited by John Martin. New York: Dodd, Mead, 1903.

Riddle, Maxwell. *The Springer Spaniel.* Chicago: Judy, 1951.

Watson, James. *The Dog Book.* New York: Doubleday, 1909.

Veterinary Sources

Campbell, William E. *Behavior Problems in Dogs.* Goleta, California: American Veterinary Publications, Inc., 1975.

Carlson, Delbert G., D.V.M., and James M. Giffin, M.D. *Dog Owner's Home Veterinary Handbook.* New York: Howell, 1980.

Corley, E. A., D.V.M., and G. G. Keller, D.V.M. *Hip Dysplasia, A Guide for Dog Breeders and Owners.* Columbia, Missouri: Orthopedic Foundation for Animals, 1989.

National Animal Poison Control Center, College of Veterinary Medicine, University of Illinois. 1-900-680-0000 ($20.00 for first 5 minutes, plus $2.95 for each additional minute, $20.00 minimum) or 1-800-548-2423 Credit cards only, ($30.00/case).

Vine, Louis L., D.V.M. *Your Dog, His Health and Happiness.* New York: Prentice, 1971.

Whitney, Leon F., D.V.M., and George D. Whitney, D.V.M. *The Complete Book of Dog Care.* New York: Doubleday, 1985.

Associations

American Kennel Club, 51 Madison Ave., New York, NY 10010.

Canadian Kennel Club, 89 Skyway Ave., Ste. 100, Etobicoke, Ontario M9W6R4, Canada

English Springer Spaniel Field Trial Association, Inc., Marie Anderson, Corresponding Secretary, 29512 47th Ave. S., Auburn, WA 98001.

United Kennel Club, 100 East Kilgore Rd., Kalamazoo, MI 49001-5598.

Index

Index

Index

Index

BARRON'S PET REFERENCE BOOKS

Barron's Pet Reference Books are and have long been the choice of experts and discerning pet owners. Why? Here are just a few reasons. These indispensable volumes are packed with 35 to 200 stunning full-color photos. Each provides the very latest expert information and answers questions that pet owners often wonder about.

——— BARRON'S PET REFERENCE BOOKS ARE: ———

AQUARIUM FISH
AQUARIUM PLANTS MANUAL
BEFORE YOU BUY THAT KITTEN
BEFORE YOU BUY THAT PUPPY
THE BEST PET NAME BOOK EVER
CARING FOR YOUR OLDER CAT
CARING FOR YOUR OLDER DOG
CARING FOR YOUR SICK CAT
THE CAT CARE MANUAL
CIVILIZING YOUR PUPPY
COMMUNICATING WITH YOUR CAT
COMMUNICATING WITH YOUR DOG
THE COMPLETE BOOK OF PARAKEET CARE
DICTIONARY OF AQUARIUM TERMS
DOG TRAINING WITH A HEAD HALTER
EDUCATING YOUR DOG
THE EXOTIC PET SURVIVAL MANUAL
FEEDING YOUR PET BIRD
FUN AND GAMES WITH YOUR DOG
GUIDE TO A WELL-BEHAVED CAT
GUIDE TO A WELL-BEHAVED PARROT

HAND-FEEDING AND RAISING BABY BIRDS
HEALTHY CAT, HAPPY CAT
HEALTHY DOG, HAPPY DOG
HEY PUP, LET'S TALK!
HOME FARM HANDBOOK, THE
HOP TO IT: A Guide To Training Your Pet Rabbit
THE HORSE CARE MANUAL
HOW TO TEACH YOUR OLD DOG NEW TRICKS
IDEAL PUPPY, THE
ILLUSTRATED GUIDE TO 140 DOG BREEDS
INDOOR CATS
LIZARD CARE FROM A TO Z
101 QUESTIONS YOUR CAT WOULD ASK
101 QUESTIONS YOUR DOG WOULD ASK
1000 PHOTOS OF AQUARIUM FISH
THE SECRET LIFE OF CATS
SHOW ME
THE ULTRAFIT OLDER CAT
TRAINING YOUR PET RAT
THE TROPICAL MARINE FISH SURVIVAL MANUAL
. . . AND MANY MORE

Books may be purchased at your local bookstore, or by mail from Barron's. Enclose check or money order for the total amount plus sales tax where applicable and 18% for postage and handling (minimum charge $5.95). Prices subject to change without notice.

Barron's Educational Series, Inc., 250 Wireless Boulevard, Hauppauge, New York 11788. For sales information call toll-free: 1-800-645-3476.

In Canada: Georgetown Book Warehouse, 34 Armstrong Avenue, Georgetown, Ontario L7G 4R9. Call toll-free: 1-800-247-7160.
Order from your favorite bookstore or pet shop.
Visit our website at: www.barronseduc.com   (#64) R 12/99

BARRON'S COMPLETE LINE OF DOG BREED OWNER'S MANUALS

Barron's *Complete Pet Owner's Manuals* include an extensive line of titles that provide basic information on individual canine breeds. The author of each manual is an experienced breeder, trainer, or vet. Each book is filled with full-color photos and instructive, high-quality line art. You'll learn what you need to know about each breed's traits, and get advice on purchasing, feeding, grooming, training, breeding, and keeping a healthy and happy dog.

Afghan Hounds
ISBN 0-7641-0225-7

Airedale Terriers
ISBN 0-7641-0307-5

Akitas
ISBN 0-7641-0075-0

Alaskan Malamutes
ISBN 0-7641-0018-1

American Eskimo Dogs
ISBN 0-8120-9198-1

**American Pit Bull &
Staffordshire Terriers**
ISBN 0-8120-9200-7

Australian Cattle Dogs
ISBN 0-8120-9854-4

Australian Shepherds
ISBN 0-7641-0558-2

Basset Hounds
ISBN 0-8120-9737-8

Beagles
ISBN 0-8120-9017-9

**Bernese and Other
Mountain Dogs**
ISBN 0-8120-9135-3

Bichon Frise
ISBN 0-8120-9465-4

Bloodhounds
ISBN 0-7641-0342-3

Border Collies
ISBN 0-8120-9801-3

Boston Terriers
ISBN 0-8120-1696-3

Boxers
ISBN 0-8120-9590-1

Brittanys
ISBN 0-7641-0448-9

Bulldogs
ISBN 0-8120-9309-7

Cairn Terriers
ISBN 0-7641-0638-4

**Cavalier King
Charles Spaniels**
ISBN 0-7641-0227-3

Chesapeake Bay Retrievers
ISBN 0-7641-0657-0

Chihuahuas
ISBN 0-8120-9345-2

Chow Chows
ISBN 0-8120-3952-1

Cocker Spaniels
ISBN 0-7641-1034-9

Collies
ISBN 0-8120-1875-3

Dachshunds
ISBN 0-8120-1843-5

Dalmatians
ISBN 0-7641-0941-3

Doberman Pinschers
ISBN 0-8120-9015-2

Dogs
ISBN 0-8120-4822-9

English Springer Spaniels
ISBN 0-8120-1778-1

The German Shepherd Dog
ISBN 0-8120-9749-1

German Shorthaired Pointers
ISBN 0-7641-0316-4

Golden Retrievers
ISBN 0-8120-9019-5

Great Danes
ISBN 0-8120-1418-9

Great Pyrenees
ISBN 0-7641-0734-8

Greyhounds
ISBN 0-8120-9314-3

Huskies
ISBN 0-7641-0661-9

Irish Setters
ISBN 0-8120-4663-3

Jack Russell Terriers
ISBN 0-8120-9677-0

Keeshonden
ISBN 0-8120-1560-6

Labrador Retrievers
ISBN 0-8120-9018-7

Lhasa Apsos
ISBN 0-8120-3950-5

Maltese
ISBN 0-8120-9332-1

Mastiffs
ISBN 0-7641-0762-3

Miniature Pinschers
ISBN 0-8120-9346-1

Miniature Schnauzers
ISBN 0-8120-9739-4

Mutts
ISBN 0-8120-4126-7

Newfoundlands
ISBN 0-8120-9489-1

Old English Sheepdogs
ISBN 0-7641-0735-6

Pekingese
ISBN 0-8120-9676-2

Pomeranians
ISBN 0-8120-4670-6

Poodles
ISBN 0-8120-9738-6

Pugs
ISBN 0-8120-1824-9

Retrievers
ISBN 0-8120-9450-6

Rottweilers
ISBN 0-7641-1033-0

Saint Bernards
ISBN 0-7641-0288-5

Samoyeds
ISBN 0-7641-0175-7

Schipperkes
ISBN 0-7641-0337-7

Schnauzers
ISBN 0-8120-3949-1

Shar-Pei
ISBN 0-8120-4834-2

Shetland Sheepdogs
ISBN 0-8120-4264-6

Shih Tzus
ISBN 0-8120-4524-6

Siberian Huskies
ISBN 0-8120-4265-4

Small Dogs
ISBN 0-8120-1951-2

Spaniels
ISBN 0-8120-2424-9

Vizslas
ISBN 0-7641-0321-0

**Welsh Corgis: Pembroke
and Cardigan**
ISBN 0-7641-0557-4

**West Highland White
Terriers**
ISBN 0-8120-1950-4

Whippets
ISBN 0-7641-0312-1

Yorkshire Terriers
ISBN 0-8120-9750-5

Barron's Educational Series, Inc.
250 Wireless Blvd., Hauppauge, NY 11788 • To order toll-free: 1-800-645-3476
In Canada: Georgetown Book Warehouse • 34 Armstrong Ave.,
Georgetown, Ont. L7G 4R9 • Order toll-free in Canada: 1-800-247-7160
Or order from your favorite bookstore or pet store
Visit our web site at: www.barronseduc.com

(#110) 9/99